Bright Ideas

Teacher Handbooks
Handbooks
Art and Craft
Techniques

D1458828

Published by Scholastic Publications Ltd,
Marlborough House, Holly Walk,
Leamington Spa, Warwickshire CV32 4LS

© 1988 Scholastic Publications Ltd
Reprinted 1989

Contributors: Malcolm Appleby, Clive
Butler, Mary Lack, Wendy Hawkin, Pauline
Rayner, Mary Smart, Maureen Greenland,
Chris Vesey, Eileen Lowcock, Roland Smith,
Sandra Goode

Edited by Jackie Cunningham-Craig and
Jane Hammond
Sub-edited by Melissa Bellamy
Photographs by Richard Butchins
Illustrated by Ginny Crow and Roy Mole
Advised by Eileen Lowcock

Printed in Great Britain by Ebenezer Baylis,
Worcester

ISBN 0 590 70877 5

Front and back covers: photographs by Martyn
Chillmaid; designed by Sue Limb; work by children of
Coton End Middle School, Warwick

Contents

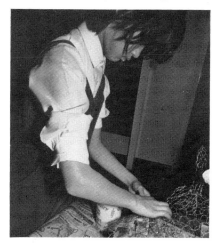

Contents

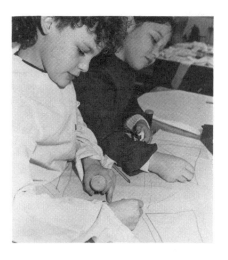

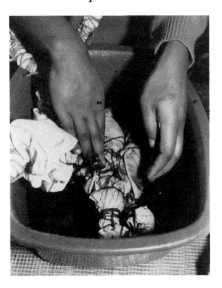

Introduction

Art & Craft Techniques, like all the *Bright Ideas Teacher Handbooks*, is designed as a handbook for teachers, and not a direct reference book to be used with the children in the classroom. The information should be absorbed, digested by the teacher, and then passed on to the children.

Where traditional techniques are strictly adhered to in early learning processes, creativity is stifled. The techniques described here are designed to be used as a resource for you to dip into and pass on to the children when they reach the appropriate stage in creative development.

To encourage creative expression, and experimentation with materials, and to allow children to develop their own ideas, should be your prime motivation, suggesting and demonstrating a new technique to the children at the appropriate time to explore and experiment with it

before introducing the next technique.

The chapters or individual techniques have been written by craft experts and primary school teachers, several of whom are also regular contributors to *Art & Craft* magazine. The subjects, methods and techniques have, therefore, all been thoroughly tested by experienced teachers in a variety of primary schools.

Each craft has its place in the spectrum of the curriculum, and none should be singled out as being more important or more relevant than another. Creative work can be seen in terms of those cell modules, each linked to another, since no craft can be worked in isolation without borrowing the skills used for another. This cross reference is not restricted to craft skills alone: children develop the skills of manipulation, co-ordination, judgement, decision-making, and so on, through creative work, but

subjects such as maths, geography, history and craft skills for clarification and illustration.

Drawing skills should be encouraged so that children can communicate their thoughts and feelings more effectively. An important function of drawing is that it gives children the opportunity to discover the world around them. Through drawing from life, they are encouraged to analyse, investigate and explore their attempts to produce a drawn image.

Through the use of paints, fabrics and yarns, children learn about colour and texture along with the complexities of handling a variety of different materials. Here they have to experiment and learn to make decisions regarding the most suitable material to choose for the project in hand.

The main objectives of working with clay are to develop design skills, manipulative powers and an awareness of the beauty and form which can be achieved. Manipulative skills are continually being extended as each technique adds another process for hands and minds to understand and master. An aesthetic awareness is developed through the use of colour and continual practice in colour harmony.

Making 3-D models provides considerable scope and plays an important part in the curriculum from pre-school years. Not only do children have to consider the question of shape, size and substance, but also colour, line and texture.

Spinning, weaving and dyeing also help to fulfil the need for children to express themselves. They provide a range of valuable learning experiences and encompasses many other subjects across the curriculum.

Through printing, very young children and those who are not yet confident at drawing can print shapes on paper to form patterns and gain an understanding of rhythm and symmetry.

Pattern can be found wherever we look, so by studying patterns children will learn the difference between pattern and design, and become more aware of their environment.

Using yarns for knitting and crochet offers children the opportunity to experiment with an endless variety of colours and textures, whether they be in the yarn itself or created by a stitch pattern. These techniques are ideal for group activities, as quite small pieces of work of varying standards may be joined together to form a large piece such as a wall-hanging or a soft sculpture.

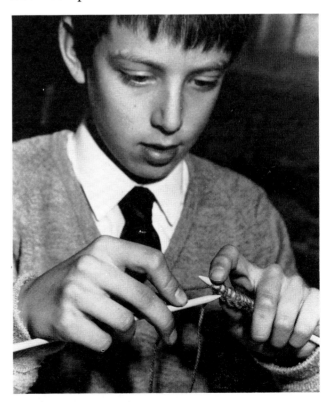

Drawing

Drawing

INTRODUCTION

Drawing skills should be encouraged so that children can communicate more of their thoughts and feelings about their world effectively, and can form a good foundation for expression in other art media.

Communication

From an early age, children use drawing and painting to communicate – before the

written word and sometimes even the spoken word. Developing from the very rudimentary marks made by young children to the kinds of symbols older children use in maps or scientific diagrams, drawn images are used to communicate a whole range of information.

Often a child's first response to an experience is an emotional one, shown perhaps in use of colour. At a very young age, lack of written or spoken language means that a drawn response to feelings is the only means of expression available.

Investigation

One very important function of drawing is the opportunity it gives children to discover the world around them. Presenting children with an object or environment to draw encourages them to analyse, investigate and explore in their attempts to produce a drawn image.

Illustrating and recording

Drawing is also a means for children to deepen their knowledge of a particular subject. Think about historical or geographical topics and how children record information in the form of illustrations. By illustrating they are able to engage with the topic much more closely and make the process more effective.

Information can be recorded in the form of drawings.

Starting points

When a child makes a drawing, he must consider four elements – colour, tone, line and texture. It is also important to realise that a drawing of an object or scene is not a copy but an *analogy*; it is representing in one material what exists in another.

3

Stimuli and materials

For a child to carry out a drawing activity effectively, he must have access to a range of good quality material, so that the texture and character of the object can be more accurately recorded.

Collections of visually exciting objects should be available, such as tree roots, an old typewriter, knotted and frayed rope, uniforms, headgear, bark, clock mechanisms, shells, fossils, feathers, plants, rocks etc.

Pencils should range from 4H, which produces a very faint hard line, to 4B, which is darker and has a more crumbly texture. At the centre of the scale lies HB, which is the most commonly used type of lead. Care should be taken not to drop the pencils on the floor, as this will shatter the lead inside and ruin them.

Charcoal can be bought in many different forms, such as pencils, scene-painters and graphite, but it is easier to handle in stick form, as it can be broken down by the children into easily manageable pieces. However, charcoal can smudge easily and, in inexperienced hands, can be very messy!

Some children find ball-point pens and crayons easier to work with than the more traditional implements like pencils and willow charcoal. Crayons (pencil and wax), pastels and chalks give the children a more exciting range of colour to work with.

Provide powder and watercolour paints, Indian ink and a range of coloured inks. Tone and shading are difficult to achieve with inks unless cross-hatching and varied thicknesses of line are used. However, this should not dissuade more adventurous pupils from trying these techniques.

Use a fixative on finished artwork to prevent smudging, especially with pencil, charcoal and soft pastel work. A less expensive alternative to professional fixative is scentless hairspray. Ensure that the children are supervised when using fixatives and that the classroom is well-ventilated, as inhalation can be dangerous.

Children using fixatives must be supervised.

Have plenty of erasers in stock, especially plastic ones, which are most effective in erasing soft pastels. An important aspect of learning to draw is to amend and correct your mistakes continually.

Encourage the children not to be heavy-handed with the lines they draw or their rubbings out; it will only result in dark gashes, smudges and holes across the paper and will make their work look untidy.

A range of papers should be available to enable children to choose the one that is most suitable for their needs.

Finally, to help children with close observation and to stimulate imagination, a selection of the following would be useful:
- viewfinders
- magnifying glasses
- coloured lenses or gelatines
- dark glasses
- distorting glass bottles

A cardboard viewfinder is invaluable for helping the child to focus his attention on a subject, by cutting out much of the surrounding, distracting details.

A viewfinder can easily be made from a large piece of card with a hole, 17 cm × 12 cm, cut out of the centre. This size is handy for both indoor and outdoor use.

Discussion

When children draw, they must make decisions about which medium to use, and how to shade a particular area or represent a texture, so it is necessary for a good deal of discussion to take place. This is especially true if they are asked to produce images of subjects outside the normal range of experiences, such as the jungles of South America, the Romans, or life on Mars, when discussion will help to clarify problems and stimulate ideas.

A viewfinder helps to focus attention on a subject.

Experience

When children are asked to record a subject such as a flower, bird or building, allow plenty of time for them to look, assess, analyse and discover the qualities of the subject. For example, only by handling an animal can children beome aware of its smell, texture, warmth and physical qualities. They can then bring the knowledge they have acquired through handling objects and creatures into their images by showing the furry texture of a rabbit, the spiky appearance of a conker or the smoothness of a leaf.

Children need time to study a subject for detail.

Using the environment is another way of giving children these first-hand experiences of the world in which they live. No matter where the school is, there is always a natural or man-made environment for children to explore through drawing and painting.

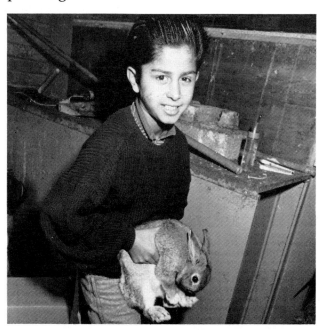

Children can get to know their subject by handling it.

Making a drawing

Qualities of line and texture

In this activity children should have
experience of using tools other than
traditional drawing implements such as
pencils or pens to make marks of varying
qualities.

Ink can stain clothing, so children
should be fairly adept at using drawing
implements. However, younger children
could carry out this activity if a suitable
water-based ink is used and they wear
protective clothing.

Provide the children with a range of
materials, such as grass, twigs, sponge,
burnt wood, cotton buds, pine cones and
matchsticks, Indian or coloured ink, and
cartridge paper (A3-sized).

Fold the cartridge paper to form eight
rectangles. Encourage the children to use
the various objects to create different types
of line with the ink in each small rectangle,
exploring the qualities of line and texture.

Get the children to draw small objects
from observation, such as bark, flowers,
grasses and items which have particularly
strong linear qualities, again using ink and
the found objects.

Working on a large scale using paint
rather than ink is a useful follow-up activity,
encouraging children to be more expansive
in their responses.

Exploring linear quality (1)

This activity enables children to explore the properties of line in the environment.

With help in the initial stages, even young children can attempt it. Older children should be able to carry it out independently.

Use kitchen and cartridge paper, thick black wax crayons, drawing inks, thin brushes, pens and charcoal.

To help children to see the linear qualities of an object, ask them to collect rubbings using the thick wax crayon and kitchen paper. The linear qualities will be revealed because the rubbing picks out the essential characteristics of the object.

Children can then attempt to copy these rubbings and extend them using drawing inks, pens or charcoal.

Children could then experiment with printing such images. String prints are particularly effective in highlighting the linear qualities of objects.

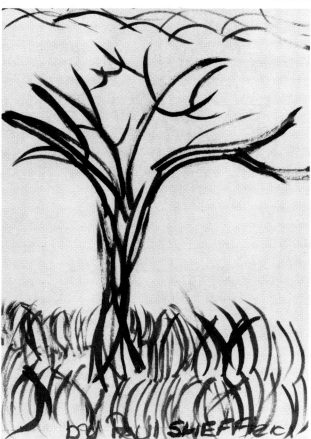

An observational drawing showing linear qualities.

Exploring linear quality (2)

Children should be given the opportunity to explore the characteristics of different drawing media.

Your choice of media for this activity will depend on the age of the children. For example, younger children may need large, chunkier pencils and crayons. However, the activity can be carried out across the age range.

Use materials such as charcoal (compressed, scene-painters, willow and pencils), pastels (soft and oil), biros, ink and brush, Conté crayons, a range of pencils (4B-4H), chalk, graphite sticks and felt-tipped pens, and provide A3-sized white cartridge paper and neutral-coloured sugar-paper.

Fold the white paper into eight rectangles and ask the children to create different effects in each section with either one or a combination of the drawing media. Then use a neutral-coloured paper and ask

the children to explore the differences when working on a non-white background. Does it change the quality of the marks?

With experience of a range of drawing media (colour and black and white) in an experimental situation, the children should be ready to attack a piece of observational work. Encourage them to mix media to help solve some of the problems raised in drawing objects.

Tonal quality

This activity will help children to appreciate tonal qualities in drawings. It is probably more suitable for children aged nine to eleven.

Provide small newspaper photographs, a range of pencils (4H-4B), cartridge paper and a card viewfinder.

It is easier to approach the examination of tone in drawing by using an image which has easily accessible tonal qualities, such as a newspaper photograph.

Tonal qualities in a newspaper photo are reproduced.

Ask the children to isolate part of a photograph using the viewfinder and to copy the tonal qualities on to the paper. It may be helpful to get them to square up both the photograph and their paper, so that they can work on a square at a time and enlarge their image.

This activity can be carried out using only HB pencils, but a range of grades makes it easier for children to differentiate between the tones.

Children could then examine their photographs under a magnifying glass to discover that the tones are made up of different denstities of dots. They could attempt this themselves by creating monochrome pictures, then they could try it in colour, using a primary colour and black and white, trying to match the tonal relationships in their photograph.

This activity could lead on to looking at the work of Seurat, who used dots of colour to produce his pointillist paintings.

Light and shade

The aim of this activity is to give children experience of using tones in an observational drawing.

Older children will probably have more success with this activity, but it might be useful to give younger children the experience, too, as it provides an opportunity for discussion.

Use simple, solid geometrical shapes, a strong light source (desk lamp), cartridge paper and pencils. Set up a still life with some simple, plain objects, such as cubes, cuboids, pyramids and cones, in front of a plain backdrop. The light source should be placed to one side so that the faces are highlighted and accentuated.

Ideally this activity should be carried out with a small group of children positioned so that they all have a good, clear view of the still life.

Before they begin work, talk about how the arrangement appears to change as the light source is moved around, creating new shadows and highlights. Perspective could be introduced by talking about how the objects appear to get smaller as they are moved further away from the viewer. This presents children with a real drawing problem to solve.

Emphasise light and shade using a strong light source.

Using coloured filters on the light source offers an opportunity for children to experiment with colour tones, while concentrating on the shadows created rather than the objects can produce some interesting drawings in colour or monochrome.

Shading clearly shows the 3-D nature of the shapes.

Degrees of tone

This activity gives children the opportunity to produce and explore a tonal scale. The youngest children in a primary school can attempt this activity, but even older children sometimes need this kind of exercise to refresh their memories.

You will need a neutral-coloured (oatmeal) sugar-paper, and black and white powder paints. Ask the children to put an area of white paint in one corner of the paper. Then, by gradually adding small amounts of black, get them to work towards the opposite corner, painting a stripe each time. They should have a picture with a range of greys at the end of the activity.

This could be done in reverse, but whereas only a tiny amount of black needs to be used to alter the tone, much more white is required to achieve a similar change.

The children could then try to paint simple patterns or a still life using only black and white and the intermediate tones.

They could also experiment by adding black to a primary colour and painting strips, and then adding white in a similar way to the activity outlined above. This could lead to an imaginative piece of work on a given theme, such as 'The red planet', 'The blue room', etc.

Texture (1)

Children need the opportunity to explore the potential of various drawing media in showing the tactile properties of objects.

Much depends on how much experience children have had of a range of drawing media, but from the middle years of the primary school it should be an activity which children can carry out successfully.

Use cartridge and coloured papers, inks, oil and soft pastels, charcoal, graphite, pencils, biros, coloured pencils, and wax crayons. A variety of papers should be provided as the texture of the paper may help to enhance the drawn textures.

Get the children to discuss a range of textures and help them to collect a word bank. This provides a useful starting point, especially if examples of the various surfaces are available. Encourage the children to experiment with the media to create a variety of textures chosen from the list they have collected.

They could then compose a purely imaginative scene including their chosen textures and using the drawing media available.

Using powder paints to create a tonal scale.

An imaginary scene drawn from different textures.

Play a game of 'guess the texture'. Using a 'feely' bag with a number of different textures inside, ask the children to draw representations of the textures they feel, not the objects themselves.

All the drawings could then be displayed with the textures.

By doing this the children begin to learn from one another, as they see how each individual response is different. Even for young children, this approach could be a useful introduction to the idea of drawn textures.

Texture (2)

Having explored the idea of drawn textures, the children can put these to some practical use by drawing objects with various textures.

Even young children should be able to show some indication of the textural qualities of an object, such as the feathers on a bird. The more experiences the children have with different drawing media and their ability to reproduce various textures, the more sophisticated their responses will be.

Use the materials from the previous activity, plus a range of objects such as stuffed animals, shells, rope, bark, slices of cabbage or other vegetables.

As in the previous activity discussion is the essential first step to bring out the full range of vocabulary and ideas. The children can then choose one of the objects and attempt a graphic representation of its textural qualities.

During the activity, discussion should be encouraged between individual children and the teacher, and amongst the children themselves, to help solve any problems which may arise. Again, a sharing of experiences and images at the end of the activity will enable the children to learn from one another.

Try limiting the objects to similar kinds of texture to emphasise the possibilities of particular media. Some textures, such as hair or scales, may produce different kinds of emotive response in children, providing a starting point for a piece of imaginative artwork.

3D texture

In this activity the children will have an opportunity to use two different kinds of art media – clay and drawing materials – to relate textural qualities in modelling and drawing. It could be adapted for almost any age, depending on their level of experience and familiarity with different media.

Textural qualities of a plant are represented here.

Materials should include clay, boards, blindfolds, and a range of drawing media and papers. The idea is that the children produce a 'walk' for their finger through a variety of textures made in a piece of clay (about the size of two tennis balls). However, while creating their walk, they should be blindfolded and the finished piece moved out of sight before they remove the blindfolds.

After cleaning up the children should try to draw their walk, using the various drawing materials to represent the different textures they created in clay. Then the drawings and clay walks can be compared to see how similar they are.

The children could then make an observational drawing of their clay walks and its variety of textures.

Shape

This activity will help children to grasp one of the essential characteristics of objects – their shape – and how this can affect responses to pictures.

Children will be experimenting with geometrical shapes and the different effects which can be achieved using specific shapes. It is therefore helpful if they have had plenty of experience in identifying geometrical shapes.

Rulers, pencils, thick felt-tipped pens and cartridge paper should be provided. Ask the children to produce two pictures using the same colours but a different grouping of geometric shapes in each. For instance, in one they may use circles and squares, whilst in the other the predominant shape is triangular. They should then write down their responses to their own and other children's work. This will help them to appreciate how shape can

Continue the exploration of texture using clay and relating the finished artefacts to drawings. The stimulus could be imaginary (a spiky monster), or taken from the environment.

Experimentation and exploration with other kinds of modelling material, such as plaster or Plasticine, will help the children to appreciate the textural qualities of objects around them.

affect the emotive response of the viewer to a picture.

Using the same combination of shapes but a different colour can help children to see how colour is also important.

Children need to learn how to use different shapes.

'Negative' shape

Accuracy and detail in the children's drawings can be improved if they are aware of 'negative' shapes – that is the space around the object or a group of other shapes.

The first part of the activity could be attempted by quite young children as it involves experimentation with simple ready-made shapes. However, the second part would be better attempted with older children.

Use simple card shapes such as letters, and provide cartridge paper, felt-tipped pens, pencils and objects for still life.

Using the shapes, ask the children to prepare a simple arrangement on the cartridge paper and draw round it. The shapes can overlap.

It is then important to discuss the shapes which have been formed between the simple motifs. These could be shaded with one colour, and then the motifs highlighted with another. This will help to emphasise the possibilities of pattern-making.

Set up a still life with a wide variety of

objects against a plain background. The children should be equipped with pencil and cartridge paper. Ask them to draw the shapes of the spaces between the objects. If they are accurate, the objects in the still life will appear as they draw the space around them. The area between the objects can then be shaded using pencil or graphite.

This activity forms a very good basis for print-making activities. Examples of wallpapers, for instance, could be looked at and different shapes identified. The children could then design their own motif to print.

Using the environment

It is important to use first-hand experiences when you involve children in the drawing process. This section outlines some approaches to making the most of the environment for creative work.

Exploring the school and built environment

These activities encourage children to explore and look closely at their environment by carrying out some simple information-collecting tasks. With adaptation, almost any age group should be able to carry them out.

Get the children to go round the school or local environment and look for pattern in what they see. They should be looking for bricks, tiles, windows, flagstones, etc, and making annotated drawings of them as a basis for later work in the classroom.

Using kitchen paper and thick wax crayons, the children can make a collection of different textures in the environment. These could be turned into a 'dictionary' of

One view of a part of the school building.

The most important aspects of school are the adults and children who make up the community. So children could make another collection of drawings, this time of their friends and adults who help them (teachers, cleaners, dinner ladies, caretaker, etc). It is best to attempt these in pencil first, with further work in paint or pastels. Before any work is carried out, discuss proportion and the relationship between different parts of the body (eyes, nose, ears, mouth, etc).

A portrait of Debbie by her friend Andrea.

textures which could also include their own drawn attempts at conveying texture (see 'Texture 1' and 'Texture 2' on pages 9–10).

The children could make a collection of drawings showing different views of the school interior and exterior. These should be annotated with information about colour, texture, form, etc. A viewfinder may be helpful in narrowing down the view for the child, or show them how to use the ready-made viewfinders in the environment, such as doors, windows, etc.

Collecting patterns could lead on to abstract paintings or print-making activities, while the textures could be

Another view of the classroom environment.

A print inspired by one small aspect of the environment.

followed up by print-making (Polyblocks are good for this) or collage work with scrap materials like fabric, string, wood shavings, etc. There is also much to be gained from working with modelling materials like clay, plaster or Plasticine, perhaps making models of the environment or members of the school community.

A better place to live

The children should have gathered quite a bit of information in the form of images and language about the environment. In this activity they are encouraged to consider some aspect of it critically.

Improving the environment is a positive and practical way to use drawing skills.

Ask the children to choose an area inside or outside the school which they think can be improved, and make drawings of it. They could then attempt some simple designs to alter the appearance of their chosen location. From their drawings they could make models showing their improvements.

In most schools you will find a wall area which could be improved, either inside or outside the building. This would be a good starting point for designing wall coverings or 3D reliefs. The children would need to try out their ideas in drawings before attempting them in other media. Printed wall-coverings using block or screen printing would be suitable for internal walls, whilst outside they could try temporary reliefs by making up small tiles in clay and taking plaster impressions of them. Once these are assembled, protect them with paint or polyurethane.

The children could look closely at their own classroom, making observational drawings of it from different viewpoints. They could even lie on the floor and draw the view above them, which will create some interesting problems of perspective to solve. This activity may lead on to designing the classroom they would like to work in.

Sensory walk

An organised walk introduces the children to the natural environment, giving them the opportunity to respond to it in various ways.

You will need to take clipboards, pencils, drawing paper (A4-sized), writing paper, and several copies of a response sheet.

First ask the children to fill in the sensory response sheets as they walk along. The sheets should encourage them to respond using all their senses and to be critical about what they see.

A selection of annotated drawings should be made as the walk progresses. Encourage the children to make the drawings quickly by picking out the most important features of what they are looking at; they can make notes about the details.

This activity should produce a wide

range of linguistic and artistic responses, so children could follow it up by writing prose or poetry about the walk.

More thoughtful visual responses using pastels or paints can be made, using the notes as a reminder.

Choosing a feature

This will encourage the children to look much more closely at one feature of the natural environment and to take their drawn response into other types of media and techniques.

Any feature of the natural environment – plants, trees, insects, small creatures, pond life or birds – could be chosen for this activity. The important thing to remember is that close concentration on one feature will help the children to become more knowledgeable and sensitive to their environment.

For example, taking a tree as the focus, children can build up a profile of it in drawings and words by looking at the following aspects:
- The angle and spacing of the branches.
- Is the trunk straight or gnarled?

To focus on one feature, it must be studied closely.

- Is the trunk in one piece or does it branch?
- Is the bark smooth or rough?
- What colours are the bark and foliage?
- How thick is the trunk?
- Is there anything growing on it?

The list is by no means exhaustive. Pointing to different aspects of the chosen feature in this way will help to improve the quality of the children's responses.

Much depends on the chosen feature as to which media are used for follow-up activities. Trees, for instance, would seem to lend themselves to rugged interpretations in clay or plaster, whilst flowers could perhaps be interpreted in tissue-paper or Cellophane.

Print-making is a technique which could be used for any feature – trees, flowers or creatures. This is also an opportunity for combined group work, building up large murals with the various elements printed or painted.

Compass drawing

This activity will encourage children to draw carefully observed images of the environment. They must be able to draw quickly and to isolate important features of the landscape.

The children will need clipboards, pencils and drawing paper. Fold the paper to form four smaller rectangles. Starting with the top left-hand corner, the children produce a quick annotated drawing of the scene before them. Turning through 90°, they draw the scene in front of them in the next rectangle. The process is repeated with the other two rectangles.

The children should be able to see how the drawings relate to one another, as features at the edges of each image should be included in the next one in the series.

Use these as a basis for print-making. The finished prints will be very basic in composition, since only the main features are being reproduced but, by using different coloured inks, these elements could be highlighted.

The children could also attempt 3D representations of their drawings, using various scrap materials and paper off-cuts.

Serial drawing

This activity will enhance the children's perceptions of the environment and how the elements in it appear to change as they move through it.

The children need to have reached a proficient level of rapid drawing. As with the compass drawing activity, they need to be able to isolate the most important elements in what they see.

Again the children need clipboards, pencils and drawing paper. The drawing paper needs first to be divided into six rectangles. By following a prescribed route and stopping at six points along the way, the children should be able to build up a collection of images which, when put together, will make up a series similar to an animated cartoon. As they draw, they should pick out only the most important elements.

When they have finished, they will be able to see how elements which are not very large in one drawing become more pronounced in subsequent ones as they move nearer to the objects. Images produced in this way give the impression of movement.

By cutting up the images in order of progression, the children should be able to see how the scene changed as they walked along. To emphasise this, the major elements could be given one particular colour in each image.

Colour and painting

Colour and painting

INTRODUCTION

Children's natural curiosity about their surroundings means that there is a ready-made starting point for art education even before their first days of school.

They should be encouraged to look carefully at their environment, and provided with opportunities to express their ideas, thoughts and feelings about it by using a wide variety of materials and media.

There is a danger, however, that art and craft activities can become a hotchpotch of disjointed ideas with very little thought about the skills and techniques used, and how these might be built upon.

Painting and skill-building

We should be aiming for both consistency and continuity in our approach to painting throughout the school. The basic principles should be introduced, and then consolidated, with the introduction of further techniques as the child's confidence and mastery of the skills builds up.

However, it is important to remember that the notion of progress can sometimes be misleading. The oldest junior pupils can achieve stunning finger painting and the very youngest infants may find the challenge of painting with a small brush an interesting one. Indeed, some restrictions can provide learning structures, such as allowing the children to use only one colour plus black and white.

Children need regular opportunities to experiment with a new medium or technique, so that they have a chance to examine its potential without feeling restricted or disadvantaged. Successful use of a new technique or medium boosts a child's self-esteem and builds confidence to experiment with a further range of methods and materials.

Children of all ages should have the chance to explore and experiment with paint. At its simplest level this may involve applying dabs of paint to different surfaces to see how primary colours can be mixed to form new colours.

Ample opportunity should also be given to experiment with brushes of different sizes and other painting implements, to paint straight, curved, or jagged lines, and dragging, pushing and stippling, for example.

With all these experiments the work need not result in a 'picture'; the emphasis should be on the experiences rather than the finished product.

Similarly there should be opportunities to use a wide range of materials of varying texture, size and shape. For example, different types of paper show various effects created by the use of softer, harder, resistant or absorbent surfaces. Likewise the paint might be block, powder, watercolour or acrylic.

Technique and expression

Above all, we ought to be working towards a healthy balance between technique and expression, because in every aspect of creative art and craft both these qualities need to be present. It is often very tempting to pick up recipes for painting lessons, which make no demands whatsoever upon the children.

Experiment with different sized paintbrushes.

The experience of art education, which enables children to observe, to make decisions and to solve problems should have an impact across the curriculum. Painting has great potential for project work, apart from getting children to copy illustrations or photographs from books. It should enable them to express their ideas with art materials when other forms of communication are either inappropriate or inadequate.

Preparation

All painting stems from observation – from looking at and representing what exists. It is difficult to produce realistic pictures from the imagination; most artists find that

Encourage children to examine shape and texture first.

21

if they wish to paint such pictures they need to have studied for some time how real things look.

Therefore, before starting painting, encourage discussion and questions about the nature of the task, the objectives and the skills involved. Draw the children's attention to possible difficulties and ensure that the purpose of the activity is clear.

The children should be directed to look closely at the basic shape of the object, the surface texture (whether smooth and shiny or rough and pitted), its colour and how the light affects it. In other words, they should be concerned first of all with the underlying structure and then with the surface appearance.

It is best to start by painting something real, ideally with a sharp outline. The teacher can then discuss shapes, colours and textures in relation to something the child can see.

The more a child observes, handles and discusses the things he is going to paint, the more detailed his work will be. For example, discussions and questioning enable the child to build up a colour vocabulary and to appreciate that there are many tones of each colour.

Laying the table

The painting table should be covered with two layers of newspaper to soak up any spills, and the children ought to wear a painting overall of some description.

Supply a large piece of good quality paper for painting on and an extra strip of the same paper for the children to test out their colours as they are mixed.

The mixing palettes must be kept clean, as it is unfair to expect children to mix paints successfully in a dirty palette stained with ingrained paint.

The table itself should be flat because water-based paints tend to be difficult to control on a sloping surface.

Also try to ensure that the messy parts of an activity, such as the mixing, are kept away from the painting itself. Never let two children share the same equipment.

Make sure the children have access to a sink, as they will need to change the water

22

Newspaper and overalls protect furniture and children.

regularly. If this is not possible, store water in washing-up liquid containers, kept on the tables for mixing paint and rinsing brushes, and provide a bucket for the dirty water.

Holders containing six small individual powder paint pots are ideal and can be kept at the painting table. This is more economical than letting children spoon large quantities of powder paint straight into their palettes from the main buckets or tins.

Brushes

It is essential to offer the children a range of brushes, both small and large. House-painting brushes are also useful for covering larger areas, and for certain painting techniques, such as spatter painting.

Ensure that the children look after the brushes, which are best stored flat in a newspaper-lined tray, not in an upright container. Always keep brushes separate which are to be used for paint mixed with PVA. These need to be washed immediately after use, preferably in hot soapy water.

Good brush technique is important; children need to be shown how to hold the brush correctly and the brush strokes to employ. Scrubbing with the brushes should be discouraged as it shortens their life alarmingly.

Other methods of application

It is important to point out that brushes are not the only method of applying paint to a surface. Most children enjoy inventing and making their own painting implements, and they should be given the opportunity to experiment with such things as rags, strips of card, rollers and sponges.

Sponges, for example, offer endless opportunities for painting experiments. Rich, rough textures and special effects can be achieved when paints of different consistencies are applied with sponges of various qualities. For instance, if synthetic sponges are cut into wedges they can be used for painting lines. A damp squeezed-out sponge can be used to lighten areas of colour that have become too dark or to blend colours when painting flowers, skies or skin tones. Experimenting with different strokes, colour combinations and pressure on the sponge to create soft gradations in tone, all offer exciting possibilities. These

Experiment with various implements, such as sponges.

techniques can then be chosen by the children to complete or enhance their paintings.

Cotton buds are useful as they are easy to hold and absorbent, and they keep their shape well. They are especially useful for painting small, precise areas, such as the petals and stamens of flowers, or for suggesting the distant path in a landscape. Like sponges, they can also be used to lift off colour and soften edges.

Impressions taken from the woven surface of fabrics offer a wonderful variety of patterns. There are many suitable fabrics, including hessian, washing-up cloths, lace and binca. Fabric impressions are a useful method of depicting man-made surfaces, such as brickwork and fencing. Similarly, fur fabric is ideal for applying paint to show the subtlety of a leafy or grassy area.

Powder paint mixed to a thick consistency with paste or plaster of Paris allows children to try painting quickly with a springy blunt knife or palette knife. Thick paint, heavily applied to the surface to create a rough, uneven texture, is called *impasto*. This is ideal for representing the roughness of tree barks, rocks, animal skins and scales, and wild seascapes. Further details can easily be scratched into the paint before it dries.

Van Gogh was able to show movement by painting with thick strokes of colour, and he applied his paint very thickly, often directly from the tube. For example, his painting *Beach at Scheveningen* shows the wave patterns of the sea in thick paint.

Drawing first

Following initial discussions, children should be encouraged to draw the subject on a large scale, as it is easier to paint large areas. Pencils or white chalk are best for drawing as charcoal tends to dirty the paint.

Always demand close attention to detail in the children's drawings. If they are observing closely, their drawings will often take a good deal longer than they expect.

Always tell the children to call you to look at their work and never to bring it to you, as it may get ruined in transit. Also advise them to turn the paper round when necessary so that they do not lean on or try to work across the wet parts of their paintings.

Powder paint

Powder paint is still the most popular painting material in schools. Because it is supposed to be made to a creamy consistency, the children should be encouraged to mix their paint to the right thickness before they commit paint to paper. Remember that powder paint can also be mixed with sand, sawdust, plaster of Paris and adhesive to achieve a variety of effects. Mixing the paint with PVA helps to preserve the freshness of the colours.

If you feel that your pupils are too young to manage powder paint in its dry form, it can easily be premixed into a liquid form in bulk, and stored in plastic bottles or ice-cream containers.

Taking care

It is vital that the teacher insists on care at all stages, reminding the children that their paintings will take a long time to complete. They can become careless and spoil their painting if they are not concentrating on their work. Do not forget to let the children discuss and see each others' work, both as they are being produced and when they are completed.

Continuing discussio

Obviously, the teacher should try to stress the good parts of a piece of work. Talk, therefore, continues to be important from the very outset of a painting. Talk about the choice of subject, materials and techniques, viewpoint, framing and scale, and about the subject itself.

Colour mixing

Simple experiments with colour should always be encouraged. Children will learn much more about the characteristics and

properties of colour if they have to mix the colours themselves.

First they can discover the nature of

primary colours, and how to make shades and tints, by exploring mixing. This leads on to the creation of secondary colours.

Primary and secondary colours

Give the children a range of basic colours and allow them to explore colour mixing. Without restricting their choice too greatly, advise them not to mix more than two or three colours together, as this tends to give a muddy shade.

After a while give them a challenge: 'Can anyone make a red, a blue, or a yellow without using that colour to start with?' The children will soon discover that they can't, and you can explain that these colours are called the primary colours.

They now need the chance to explore combinations of these colours. Firstly, remembering that it is easier to mix dark paint into light, explore the effects of adding small quantities of a primary colour to white to make various tints of that colour. Similarly, add small quantities of black to a primary colour to produce various shades of that colour.

If the resulting shades and tints are cut into regular shapes, such as rectangles, circles or triangles, they can be arranged by the children from light to dark or vice versa. If an appropriately coloured head is added these shapes can become the body parts of a monster with a snake-like body. Combine the work of all the pupils to make large monsters, providing an effective and colourful display.

The secondary colours can be discovered by exploring combinations of the primary colours. For example, blue and yellow give green, red and yellow make orange, and red and blue give purple.

Families of colour can then be explored, such as how many different hues of purple can be made from different mixtures of red and blue.

The children's experiments with primary and secondary colours can be used to produce attractive pictures of rainbows – a popular subject with younger children. If the sections are drawn in wax crayon, the

Make a monster using shapes of various shades.

colours will not run into each other.

Abstract designs can be produced by drawing around and overlapping various shapes. Imagine that each object is transparent and of a primary colour so that where they overlap they will produce a secondary colour.

When mixing try to focus the discussion on the idea of lighter and darker. Coloured bottles, fruit or a piece of plain fabric draped over a chair are all subjects which lend themselves to this kind of activity because they catch light and shadow. Looking at works of art can prove profitable here; many artists did not use black, but composed dark areas in their paintings from blues, purples or browns. Children can also respond to the challenge of omitting black from their palette.

Consequently, no school really needs a great range of paint colours, as the three primary colours (plus black and white) are perhaps all that are necessary. All other colours can be mixed from these, although it is probably more helpful to provide two types of yellow, two reds and two blues. It is also important to have available much larger quantities of white than other colours.

Colour from observation

Through close observation children will discover a wide range of colours and shades, and learn how to reproduce them.

If any painting is to be based on what has been observed outside, then it is important to make field sketches which contain as much information as possible. Notes about colours can be written on the drawing, as well as any descriptions which will jog the child's memory when she is back in the classroom. For example, 'The sky near those trees is the colour of my dad's car', or 'That fence is the colour of milk chocolate.'

Brick walls provide a good opportunity for colour mixing from observation. If the children look closely, they will see that bricks are not just pure red, but have a wide range of colours within one brick, due to the use of different clays in their manufacture, the temperature at which they were fired, plus the effects of weathering, damp, mould and scratching. Once the children have matched the colours as closely as possible in paint, they could mix sand into the paint or sprinkle salt on the work while it is still wet to give a realistic rough texture to the paintings.

Reproducing colours and markings leads on to camouflage.

Candle flames are a useful source of study for a colour matching exercise, since the children should be able to observe several colours within the flame. To reproduce these observations will require careful colour mixing, which is more worth while and demanding than if they had simply been asked to paint a fire picture from memory.

Studies of animals in their habitats provide another opportunity for careful colour mixing. Unfortunately, children cannot always paint and draw animals from real life, but they can use their observational powers to paint animals or insects from colour photographs. The emphasis here is again on matching the colours as accurately as possible.

Following on from this activity, the children could discuss how their chosen creature uses camouflage to protect itself in its natural habitat. For instance, how do a tiger's stripes or a jaguar's markings help them to blend in with their surroundings? Why is it that sharks have lighter coloured underbellies and darker tops if the sea itself gets darker towards the bottom?

It is often a good idea to complete the animals in one session, and then discuss and complete the appropriate background in others. By cutting out the animal and sticking thin strips of wood or card on to the back before sticking it to the background, a 3D effect can be achieved.

Children can remember colours by making careful notes.

Colour wheels

Colour wheels are a useful way of showing the effects of mixing paints, and highlighting how colours complement each other.

First divide a circle of card into six segments and paint the top segment yellow. Miss out a segment and paint the next one blue, then miss another before painting the next segment red.

Now mix equal amounts of yellow and blue to make the secondary colour green, and fill in the blank segment between those two primary colours. Do the same for red and yellow to make orange, and red and blue to make purple.

This wheel should help the children to see that each primary colour is complemented by a secondary colour which is directly opposite on the colour wheel.

It should also show that some colours look warm and others cool. The red and orange side of the wheel looks warm, but the greens and blues appear cooler; the yellow seems warmer towards the red side and yet cooler towards the blue. Similarly, the purple which appears to be warmer towards the red looks cooler towards the blue.

Colour mixing and contrast

Studying colour mixing and contrast helps a child's understanding of colour characteristics.

If a square of one colour is placed on larger squares of various colours, then contrasts can be noted and discussed between, for example, light and dark.

Another useful exercise in colour mixing and contrast is to collect together a variety of objects of the same colour family and paint them. Tomatoes, red plums, an earthernware flower pot, a red plastic football and red scarf could be arranged together and painted to explore a variety of mixtures of one colour.

Older children might try to design and produce folding paint charts for an imaginary paint manufacturing company.

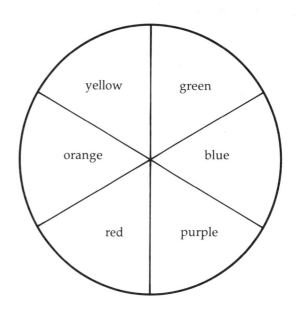

A colour wheel showing the position of the colours.

After mixing and producing a variety of colours using their previous knowledge they can give each colour a name. This, and thinking up an eye-catching slogan for their products, involves a fair amount of both language work and design.

Collect objects of the same colour and reproduce the shades.

27

Advanced colour-mixing

In completing a colour picture, children must consider scale as well as careful colour-matching.

Small cut-out parts of coloured pictures from magazines are ideal for wide-ranging and more demanding colour mixing exercises. The cut-out is stuck on to a larger sheet of plain paper and the idea is to extend it to fill this larger sheet. Mixing the colours to match those on the cut-out and planning the rest of the picture requires careful thought. The children also learn about scale during this exercise.

If additional copies of the original complete picture are available, compare these with the child's finished picture. Sometimes you will find that they have developed on uncannily similar lines.

Looking at works of art

Studying the work of an artist, whether famous or relatively unknown, is often an excellent way of trying out the techniques favoured by various art movements.

It is essential to have a good supply of materials such as prints of paintings by your chosen artists. There are numerous art appreciation books in libraries, as well as magazines covering their lives and work.

If the children are attempting to copy a painting, they will need a good colour reproduction from which to work. Using the squaring-up method if their reproduction is small, the children could then attempt to create a copy of the work. They should also try to copy, as closely as possible, the painting techniques used to complete the original. For example, they could reproduce Monet's *The Water Lily Pond* and, based on their previous experiments, show the shadows made up of blues, greens and other dark colours, without using black.

They can also use their understanding of colour mixing and close observation to paint clouds and skies more effectively. Children tend to resort to fairly characterless blue hues unless their awareness of the innumerable colours in a seemingly ordinary sky can be heightened. Some of the works by artists such as Alfred Sisley and Claude Monet of the Impressionist era illustrate various ways of successfully painting skies.

Children study prints to find out more about the techniques used by various artists.

Rousseau – contrast and observation

Most classes could gather together a sufficient number of house-plants for a group to observe and paint. This is an excellent exercise in mixing greens.

Once these have been completed, a study of the work of the French artist Henri Rousseau follows on very naturally. Many of Rousseau's paintings depict luxuriant jungle scenes, and he spent many hours observing the exotic plants in the zoological gardens of Paris to gather the basic information for his work.

Various shades of green are mixed to paint house-plants.

Rousseau always prided himself on the variety of tones he was able to introduce into each picture. One visitor to his studio claimed to have heard him say with pleasure that he was on his twenty-second shade of green.

Children readily spot common house-plants in Rousseau's pictures and enjoy trying to reproduce their own jungle scenes based on their close observation of house-plants. The addition of a jungle creature (usually a member of the cat family), as in Rousseau's paintings, completes the scene.

Studies of Rousseau's paintings will also reveal how he cleverly used small patches of complementary colours to set off the greens in his pictures. Red and orange

plants and animals are common to many of his jungle scenes.

Children will soon learn that much careful observation, discussion, colour experimentation, and an understanding of the relationships between colours, goes into producing paintings such as these.

Seurat and pointillism

A deeper understanding of how the human eye fits colours together to make a whole can be gained by looking at colour magazine pictures under a microscope. This will show, usually much to the surprise of the children, that each picture is made up of numerous tiny dots of colour which merge and overlap to produce each shade.

This discovery leads naturally to a study of the technique of pointillism. Show the children prints and photographs of paintings by Georges Seurat to illustrate this. The children could then experiment with the main pointillism techniques of dotting, scattered dashes, short vertical strokes and combined dots and dashes.

It is best not to give the children a very large piece of paper to work on first of all (A4 is large enough to begin with), because

For pointillism it is best to keep the subject simple.

trying to fill a big piece of paper with very small dots or dashes is a daunting task.

Use thick powder paint and the end of a plastic straw instead of a small brush, to build up pictures with tiny dots.

Remind the children that if the dots are spaced too far apart the effect is lost, but try not to fuse the dots too much – leave this to the viewer's eye. The features of the picture should be kept very simple; landscapes and seascapes are good starting points.

It is important that the children use various shades and tints of colour to get the best effects of light and dark, as well as to give them depth.

Pointillism does away with the linear treatment of outlines, relying instead on the careful arrangement of the dots to define shapes and masses. It is therefore essential that the children regularly stand back from their work to see the full effect of the painting, because the blending of the colours is not so apparent at close quarters.

If a larger work is attempted then larger dots or strokes can be used effectively and more detailed paintings become possible. Large dots can be made most easily using finger tips dipped into thick powder paint.

Developing a technique

Developing a particular technique can influence approaches to painting later on. Although the technique employed may only form a small part of the whole work, it could make all the difference to the end product.

Spatter painting

Spatter painting involves holding a paint-filled brush above the paper and tapping it sharply to make the paint fall in a mass of irregular spots on the paper. Paintings that require either a sense of texture or rapid movement lend themselves to spatter painting.

The technique may sound haphazard, but it takes skill and concentration to build up the colour splashes into recognisable forms. There is a challenge, too, in predicting how the colours will look when they dry.

It is always best to start by covering up the surrounding floor and furniture, as over-enthusiasm often means that the paint tends to fly everywhere.

There are three main types of spattering and it is worth trying them all so that the children can decide how best to control the paint.

Bristle brushes give the best results, and an old toothbrush or house-painting brush are readily obtainable pieces of basic equipment.

To obtain very fine spatter, use a toothbrush and fairly thick paint. Drawing a lollipop stick or an old knife across the bristles releases the paint in a shower of fine speckles. To produce a slightly heavier spatter, load the brush and tap it at an angle across the top with a finger. Spattering with watercolours on wet paper creates soft, blurred edges, and combining two colours produces some very interesting results.

The most random spatter can be made using a large brush held parallel to the paper and about 15 cm above it, and tapping if from below. This method produces the lively patterns that, for example, can resemble sea spray.

When the children come to spatter on a painting, such as a rocky landscape, it is a good idea to decide carefully where the drops are to fall. Those areas which are to be kept clear of spray can be covered by scrap paper or cloth.

Active volcanoes can be effectively illustrated by mixing powder paint and plaster of Paris together. Using the *impasto*

Spatter painting is used to create foliage for a tree.

technique, place a thick grey-coloured mix on a dark background to represent the cone of the volcano. Fiery colours mixed with the plaster of Paris represent the molten lava. This can be dribbled down the cone by tilting the paper and spattered on to the picture with thick brushes to represent showers of lava.

Sea spray can be represented by loading thick white paint on to the brush and spattering it on to the painting. As with all spatter techniques, experimenting is important. Remember that changing the distance between brush and paper varies the size of the dots.

After close observation of the many hues and colours in the foliage and branches of trees, the children could paint a basic trunk and then use the spatter technique on wet paper to show the foliage since the colours blend together to form new colours. Extra texture can be added to leaves by sprinkling salt on to the still-damp area; the drying salt crystals will create a mottled effect.

Watercolours

Creating washes

Watercolours are a notoriously difficult medium to use but excellent results can be achieved by building on a few basic techniques. Washes are the best starting point and show children how the qualities and characteristics of watercolours differ from those of the more commonly used powder paint. Washes are used to achieve an even spread of colour and to create an impression of depth through the use of different strengths of the same colour.

The paper should be white and not too large to start with. It should be clipped on a board which is then tilted at a slight angle so that the paint will run down the paper.

Working with a large brush and well-diluted paint, cover the paper with horizontal brush strokes. This first wash should be allowed to dry thoroughly before other layers of slightly more concentrated paint are applied, each time starting further down the paper. Very attractive landscapes can be achieved using this technique. For example, gradations of yellow result in desert scenes, while greens produce rolling landscapes. Further experiments in altering the colour at the different stages can produce even more interesting results.

The children could then try to paint on to a wet wash before it has fully dried, where different colours are applied and are allowed to run into one another. Tipping the paper also encourages the paint to run in different directions, although the best results often occur without any assistance.

Varying the time allowed for the first wash to dry, and experimenting with varying concentrations of paint for the second wash, are also worth trying. Painting wet on wet works especially well for stormy skies or misty abstract landscapes.

Lifting out

Following on from painting wet on wet is the technique of lifting out. This has to be carried out fairly quickly to obtain the best results and is excellent for producing skies.

Clip the paper on a board and tilt it slightly to let the wash flow down the paper. A change of colour can be introduced to make the results more interesting: for instance the children may have noticed already that the sky tends to get lighter towards the horizon. When the washes are complete any excess paint needs to be soaked up from the bottom of the sheet and then, before the washes are dry, the paper should be dabbed with crumpled tissue. This will allow the white of the paper to show through the wash as clouds in the sky.

Masking out

Yet another technique developed from watercolour washes is masking out. This involves leaving white areas of paper whilst retaining an even wash over the page. It is very effective for sails and kite outlines against a sky, or white houses on a landscape.

Areas to be left white are covered with masking tape. When all these white areas have been masked, several washes can be applied using the wet on wet and lifting out techniques to paint seas, skies and landscapes. When the work is thoroughly dry, the masking tape is removed to expose the white areas.

Use a watercolour wash as a background to a landscape.

Tissue-paper is applied to 'lift out' areas of the wash.

Resist paintings

Finally, watercolours and wax can be used together in resist paintings – a useful technique for small detail.

Although these are often done with powder paint, the more transparent nature of watercolours lends itself nicely to this technique.

Wax resist painting is based on the fact that the wax on the paper will repel the wash, creating a distinct shape which stands out from its surroundings. This is especially useful when it is difficult to show very complicated detail effectively: for example, a field of tiny poppies or the cement within a stone wall. The flowers might simply be dotted in with red wax, and the cement can be drawn in a linear pattern with wax. Washes are then laid over these, and again combinations of the previous techniques might be used to show the rough texture of the stones' surface, for instance. Using the previous experiment with spattering, the flat areas of green can be brought to life by spattering on tiny specks of lighter or darker green.

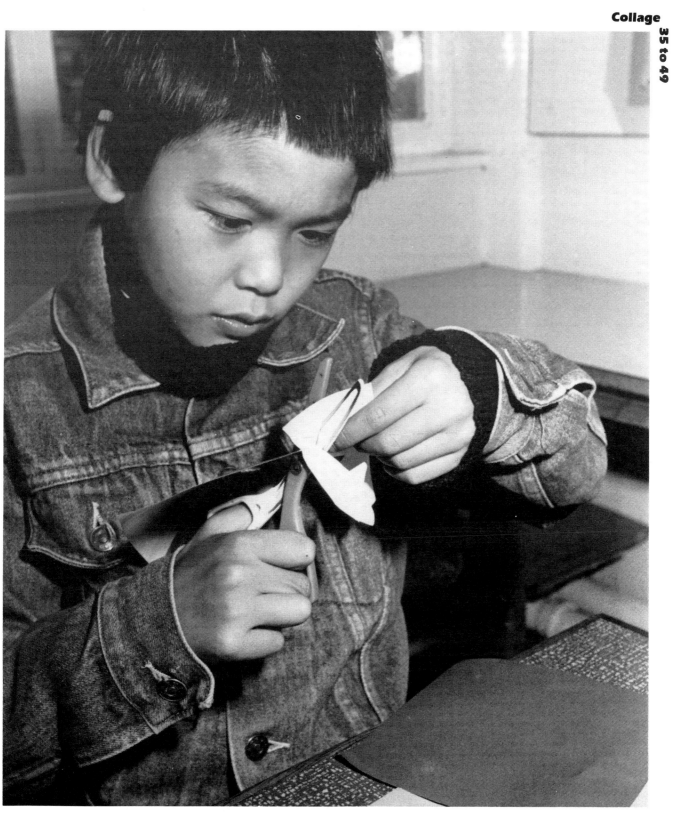

Collage

Collage

INTRODUCTION

Collage is a picture-making technique which involves sticking various materials to a background. A very wide range of materials are suitable for collage, provided that the background is strong enough, and the appropriate type of adhesive is used.

Educationally, collage is valuable because it helps children to develop an awareness of shapes, colours and textures, whilst improving motor skills. A great advantage of collage is that, apart from the background material and the adhesive, all

other materials can be scrap or left-overs. It is never too soon to start a collection of potential collage materials.

Ask children to bring in old buttons, beads, scraps of fabric from dress-making, sweet-wrappers, wood-shavings, old clothing (which can be cut up) and bits of string – just a few of the materials which are useful for collage.

Found items can make interesting raw material, too. Discarded feathers found on a country walk, empty snail shells, sea shells, dried flowers and pressed leaves all provide exciting colours, textures, and shapes.

Colour magazines are a useful source of pictures and coloured paper to use in photomontage and paper mosaics.

Store each type of item in a separate container and insist that, after each session, the remainder is put back into the correct container. This will save a great deal of time and effort in the long run, although initially it must be well-organised.

Coloured paper and fabric can also be kept in containers – a separate container for each colour. Insist that the children use up small pieces for small areas, rather than cutting into a new large piece to make a tiny shape. Encourage them to use paper and fabric economically. Left to their own devices they will cut the shape they require from the middle of a new piece of paper rather than from a corner or an edge.

Label all containers clearly, so that they can be found quickly when time is short. Ice-cream containers make cheap and practical boxes for small items, and they can be labelled with a felt-tipped marker.

Children could collect objects found on a country walk.

Sticking and drying

Non-toxic and washable PVA adhesive (the kind recommended for children) is the best type of adhesive to use for sticking most collage materials, although an ordinary paste or gum will suffice for sticking paper to paper. The most economical way to buy this is in five-litre containers. It can be decanted (by you, not the children) into small lidded containers, such as yoghurt pots or margarine tubs, for convenience and to avoid waste. Spreaders can be made from pieces of stiff card if necessary, but purpose-made plastic spreaders are much easier for children to use.

Given that you are using the right type of adhesive, it is also important to use the right amount of adhesive on the right background material. For example, a thin layer of PVA adhesive will be sufficient to secure a piece of fabric to sugar-paper, and sugar-paper is strong enough to carry fabric, but if you want a larger quantity of heavy items, perhaps large buttons or shells, then a stronger background, such as thick card or hardboard, will be needed, and the buttons and shells must be embedded in adhesive.

The collage must be left lying on a flat surface until the adhesive is completely dry; otherwise the items stuck on, especially the heavy ones, will slide off the background and be lost.

Where to start

Sometimes the starting point is dictated by a school or class project. For example, a project about birds might involve making collages on that topic. The children might choose to use an assortment of materials for their collages, trying to match the materials to the subject being depicted: feathers could be used or represented by overlapping pieces of coloured paper carefully torn to size; a nest could be depicted using straw and bits of twig and fluff.

A study of Roman Britain may involve work on mosaics, which could prompt the children to produce their own mosaics, inspired by Roman originals using seeds or squares of paper.

Encourage children to research their chosen subject.

However, the starting point may depend on the materials available. For example, a local factory might be able to supply small wood off-cuts, which might suggest a collage of a townscape, with pieces of wood used to suggest buildings.

More starting points are suggested under the headings for each type of collage. Once a starting point has been found, discuss it with the children. Show them slides and videos, arrange visits where relevant, and have plenty of books and pictures available, or ask them to do some research at home and to get books from the library.

Developing collage

Collage can be combined with other media, such as paint, crayons and simple printing to make an interesting image.

Collage materials can be dyed, too. For example, the theme for a collage might simply be 'Red'. This would involve the collection of any red materials, while other items could be dyed red. This can encourage children to see how many different shades there are of any given colour.

Allowing children to use a restricted number of colours can produce effective results, with the repetition of colours lending coherence to the collage.

Displaying the finished work

- Make borders round the finished work using pasta shapes, seeds and pulses, ribbon or braid, or add a carefully ruled border in a contrasting colour.
- Cut round the outlines of the finished items, and display all the work against contrasting-coloured or black paper. Black can be extremely attractive when bright colours have been used.
- Small collages could be stuck either side of a piece of card and suspended like a mobile.
- Collage birds could be cut from their backgrounds, stiffened if necessary, and displayed sitting on real branches. Alternatively, make a large collage of a tree and glue the birds to it, as if they are sitting on the branches.
- Make an environment using real stones, twigs and plant material, and display wildlife collages in it.
- Tiny collages could be stuck into a shiny metal lid which would look like a 'gold' or 'silver' frame.

Make sure the collages are displayed attractively.

Basic design

The simplest and one of the most effective ways to plan a picture is to use one shape placed centrally on the page and made almost large enough to fill the page. This shape can be broken down so that it contains more shapes.

Although this may seem obvious, very few children will opt for this method

Use one large shape to fill the page.

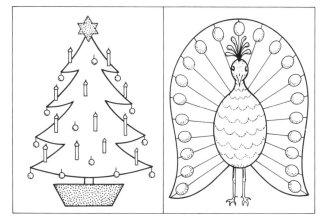

Break up the shape with decorations, or by adding detailed pattern.

without guidance. They are more likely to use as many small shapes as possible placed at random on the page. This produces an incoherent and weak design, which leaves the child asking 'How shall I fill in the gaps?' and 'What can I do in the background?'

When they see how effective the results are if they start with a large shape, they will readily adopt this method in future.

The circus

Apart from scissors and adhesive, you will need to provide background paper or card and mixed collage materials, such as fabric,

Work out proportions first; the shape should almost fill the paper.

Add the main areas of colour.

Then add details.

Other ways of dividing the picture space.

Diagonally, with one shape.

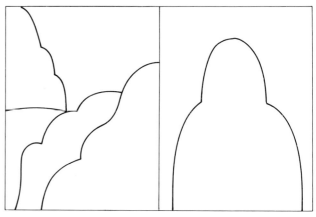

Diagonally, with more than one shape.

Subject placed centrally, going off bottom of picture space.

scrap, coloured paper, sweet-wrappers, milk-bottle tops, string (especially sisal string which makes effective lions' manes) and wool.

Begin by discussing circuses with the children. If they haven't visited one they will probably have seen one on television.

Show them as much informational material as possible and talk about it, emphasising the decorative and colourful nature of many of the acts (the clowns' make-up and costumes, the ringmaster's outfit, the trapeze artists' costumes, and so on).

Even the animals wear costumes or livery: some animals wear ruffs, circus ponies wear plumes and decorated harnesses or tack, and the accessories used, such as balls, hoops and tubs, are usually brightly coloured and patterned.

Finish the discussion by making a list

on the board of everything the children can think of in connection with the circus.

Then ask the children to choose one item each from the list to illustrate. Stress that the image should almost fill the paper; draw a diagram on the board to show what you mean.

They could depict the whole of the item, or just part of it: for example, a whole clown, showing baggy pants and enormous shoes, or just the clown's face, showing the exaggerated make-up. Explain that, whatever they choose, they must plan it first: for instance, for a clown's face, paint or cut out the basic shape of the face first, then add details to it. If they are showing the whole clown, the proportions should be worked out first, the basic colours laid in, and details added last.

Other ways of dividing the picture space are shown in the illustration, and explained by the captions.

Let the children use photographs for reference. Some will need a photograph only to find out about proportions, but others will need to copy shapes too. Make sure that they enlarge the shapes to fill their own picture area. They can do this either by making a drawing and enlarging it on a

photocopier, or by using the grid method, as follows. Draw a grid over the original picture, or draw the original on squared paper. Draw another grid with the same number of squares, but with each square larger than in the first grid. Then copy the picture square by square on to the larger grid. With young or less able children, it is sometimes necessary to use templates or patterns.

Obviously, when tackling a subject which is familiar or can be brought into the classroom, the children will be able to work from memory or from life. It may even be possible to make a special visit in order to make sketches, as with this circus activity.

Encourage the children to select materials which suggest the texture of their subject – velvet for a seal's coat, glittery or shiny materials to suggest metal, and sawdust for the circus ring. Suggest that they choose the materials before they begin, so that they can find colours which go well together, or give them a limited range of colours to use, such as primaries plus black, white and brown. Remind them to use the right amount of adhesive for their purpose (ie a thin layer to stick fabric or paper and a thick blob to secure a button).

Enlarging pictures

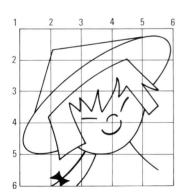

Draw a grid over the original picture.

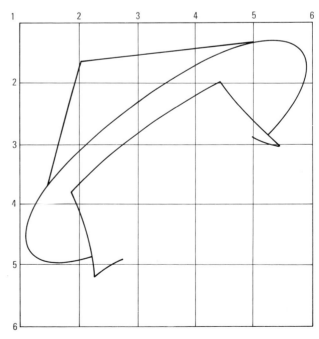

Draw a second, larger grid.
Copy the picture, square by square.

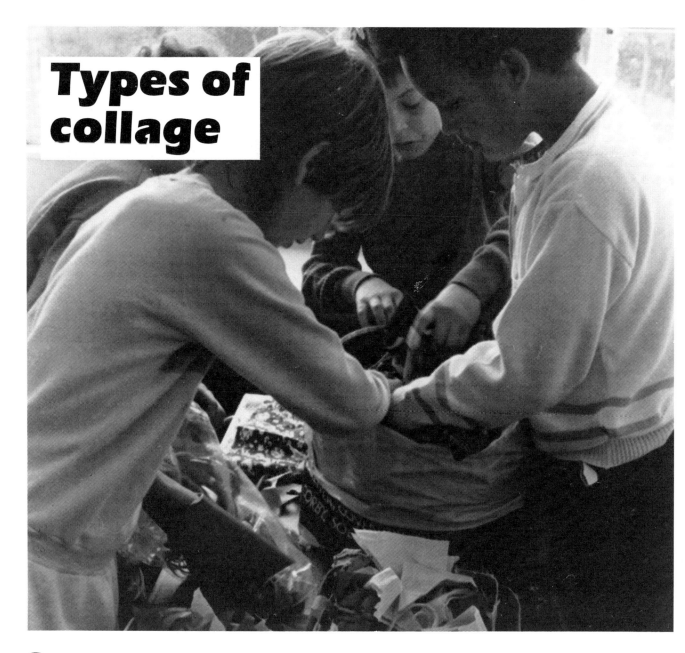

Types of collage

Scrap

Get the children to collect a variety of waste materials, such as wood veneer off-cuts, bread-bag tags, wool, fabric, leather, buttons, beads, wood-shavings, string, plant labels, pencil sharpenings, food-wrappings (clean, of course), egg trays, bristles from old brushes, in fact anything which comes to hand and can be stuck to a background. The background material must be strong if heavy items are to be used, and thick PVA adhesive, scissors sharp enough to cut fabric, and rough paper for working out ideas, must be provided.

First decide on a subject – this could arise out of work the children are doing in other subjects, or could be suggested by the materials available.

Discuss the materials, their textural qualities and shapes, and what they might be used for.

Ask the children to show you a sketch of their idea before they start on the collage. Remind them to think carefully about composition, colour and so on, laying down large areas first, and applying smaller items on top: for example, for a face, apply material for the skin first, then stick the features on top. This sounds very obvious, but invariably several of them will stick eyes directly to the background and then find they have problems with the skin.

Example

The subject in the example illustrated was suggested by a scrap of leather which was shaped like a horse's face. The heads of the girl and horse, the girl's arm and the broom are all bold shapes and fairly strong in tone. Placed together as they are, they divide the picture surface into two diagonally. The background of slabs, fence and trees were kept lighter in tone, so that they seem to recede.

The leather for the horse's head was stuck in place first, then fluffed-out sisal string was used for the mane and a bead for the eye, the teeth were cut from a plastic margarine tub, and the harness was made up from a curtain ring, some plastic binding (from a stack of roof tiles), nylon rope and used buttons.

The girl's head was added next. This was made from the lid of a margarine tub pushed into the toe from a pair of tights. Some padding was added to make the face stand away from the picture surface, then details were added: part of the plastic strip

'Girl and horse' – inspired by a scrap of leather.

from a bottle top for the mouth, a button for the nose, part of a margarine tub and felt for the eyes, wood-shavings for curls, and a bow from a box of handkerchieves. The polo neck for the jumper was cut from the ribbed top of a sock, and the body and sleeves came from the leg of the sock. The hand was cut from plastic (a margarine tub again), and covered in nylon tights fabric.

Then the broom was added, and finally the background. This could be put in last, because it was made up from several small elements rather than a few large ones. (The tiles are the plastic tags used to close bread bags.)

For this type of collage, which has some heavy items, it is essential to embed these in adhesive. The collage must be left on a flat horizontal surface to dry, so that bits don't slide off before the adhesive has dried, which takes some time if heavy items are used.

Seeds and pulses

The children will need strong card or hardboard for the background (the card from large cartons, such as packaging from electrical goods, is adequate), thick PVA adhesive and spreaders, and an assortment of seeds and pulses – as many different types, shapes and colours as possible. Remember to keep each type in a separate container, and insist that the children keep them that way. You will also need to supply pencils and rough paper.

Have plenty of reference material available, too. This should include subject matter, and examples and pictures of mosaics.

Discuss the chosen subject with the children, then introduce them to pictures of mosaics. Point out that these pictures are made up of flat areas of colour, and that each area of colour is made up of lots of small pieces. Show them the seeds and pulses, and say that you want them to use these shapes in a similar way.

Give the children rough paper on which to plan their pictures or patterns, or let them copy a mosaic picture. The plan can then be transferred to the backing material in pencil.

To attach the seeds and pulses to the backing, apply a thick layer of adhesive over the area to be covered with one particular type of seed, then embed the seeds in it. It is imperative to let the adhesive dry before moving the picture. Seeds and pulses are heavy enough to slide out of position easily if the picture is tilted.

When the design is complete, add a border also made from seeds or pulses to finish it off neatly.

Pasta shapes

Pasta shapes can be used to make patterns and borders, or in conjunction with other materials to form a picture, which then could be painted with spray paint.

Rice is useful for filling in spaces between large pasta shapes, and for contrast of colour and texture.

As for seeds and pulses, work out the design, transfer it to the (strong) backing,

apply adhesive thickly to a fairly large area, and embed the pasta and rice in it.

Sometimes there is no need to draw a design first – just look at the pasta shapes and arrange them to make a pattern. Keep shuffling them round until you have an effective pattern, then stick the pieces to the backing.

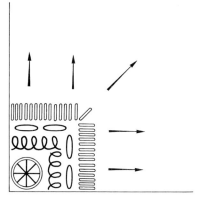

Arrange the pasta shapes to make a pattern.

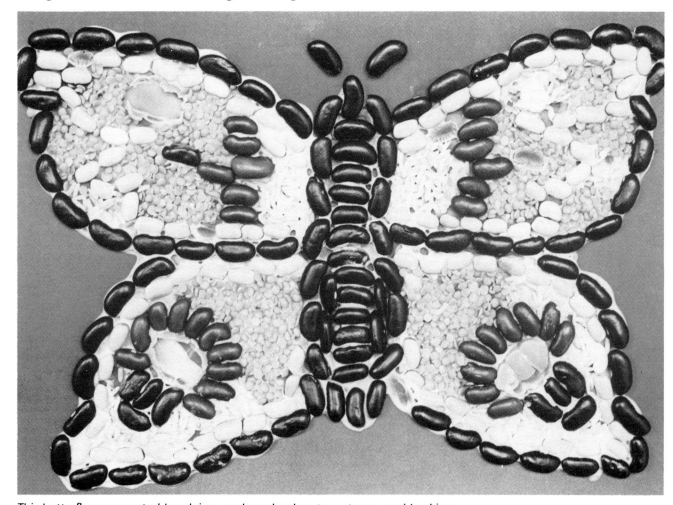

This butterfly was created by gluing seeds and pulses to a strong card backing.

44

Basic layouts for patterns.

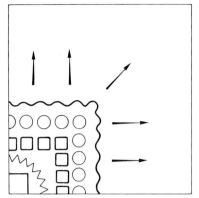

Start from one corner and work
outwards in all directions.

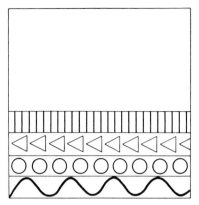

Work in strips across the page.

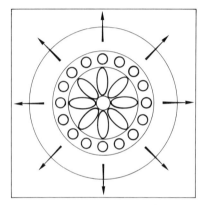

Work in concentric circles from
the centre outwards.

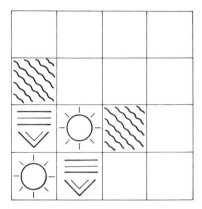

Make a grid pattern.

Natural objects

Supply the children with backing paper or
card (use card for heavy items, such as
shells), thick PVA adhesive and spreaders,
pencils, and natural materials (feathers,
leaves, pressed flowers, shells, twigs, tiny
pebbles, sheep's wool, ears of wheat, and so
on).

Use these materials either to create a
pattern or arrangement (with flowers and
leaves), or to make a picture.

To make a pattern, move the materials
round until you have a pattern you like,
possibly using one of the basic layouts
shown in the illustration.

The layout could be circular, with rings
of each type of material radiating from the
centre, or place a large shell in centre,
surrounded by a ring of tiny pebbles, then a
ring of dried flowers, and so on.

The children could divide the image
area into a grid, each part of the grid
containing a very simple arrangement, one
arrangement repeated, or several
arrangements repeated.

If the children want to create a picture,
they could either draw a picture outline or
copy one on to the backing. Decide which
materials will best fill in the spaces, then
apply adhesive in a fairly thick layer to a
small area, and fill in the area with the
chosen material. Remember that items such
as feathers, leaves and pressed flowers, can
be overlapped because they are relatively
flat. For example, if a bird is the subject of
the picture, feathers could be overlapped to
give a realistic impression; if there are no
feathers available, leaves could be
overlapped in a feather-like arrangement.

Be sure to use a strong backing,
whichever approach you use, and do apply
plenty of adhesive so that the feathers,
shells, and so on, are embedded in it. Keep
the work on a flat surface until the adhesive
is dry.

Newspapers and magazines

Supply some newspapers and colour supplements or magazines, strong paper (such as sugar-paper), PVA adhesive and spreaders, scissors and reference material.

Choose a single item as the subject, such as a bird, animal, engine, car, fish or insect. Draw the outline of the subject on to a sheet of newspaper, making it almost large enough to fill the background paper. Cut or carefully tear round the outline, and stick the newspaper shape to the background.

Build up detail in the picture by cutting or tearing more shapes from newspaper, using headlines or photographs to add depth of tone and contrast.

Use colour pages, too, to add interest, but keep colour to a minimum to encourage the use of tone. For example, for a bird, use a splash of colour in the eyes, and give it a bright plume on its head; for a face, add colour for the lips only.

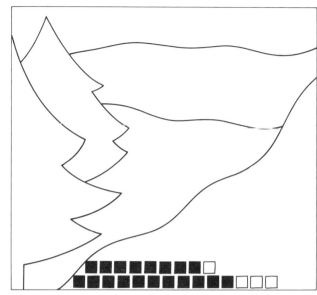

Decide on a subject, draw the outline on to backing paper, and fill in the areas with coloured squares.

Mosaic collage using colour magazines

Again the children will need a selection of colour magazines, as well as strong paper for backing, PVA adhesive and spreaders, and scissors.

Decide on a subject – preferably a single item or a landscape – and draw the outline on to the backing paper. Take coloured pages from magazines and cut them into squares, keeping different colours separate. Fill in the outlines drawn on the backing with squares of colour, placing them close together and trying to keep them evenly spaced. Details like eyes can be cut to the relevant shape rather than using squares.

Fabric

You will need plenty of scraps of fabric; the children could bring old clothes and rags to school (clean of course), as well as used buttons, ribbons, braid etc. Provide background paper, kitchen paper for making patterns, pins, PVA adhesive and spreaders. The children will also need sharp scissors, since blunt ones are extremely frustrating! Look for scissors with safe rounded points, but sharp enough to cut fabric.

Choose your topic as before, and let the

This owl was made up from scraps of newspaper.

46

children plan their pictures on a piece of rough paper. The outlines should then be drawn on the backing paper, filled in with fabric, and details added using buttons, beads, braid etc. Use fabric for background areas, or colour them with paint or wax crayon applied solidly (ie so that the background paper does not show through and make the colour appear blotchy).

Some children will work intuitively, cutting out shapes and applying them without needing an outline or pattern; allow them to do this if the work is progressing well.

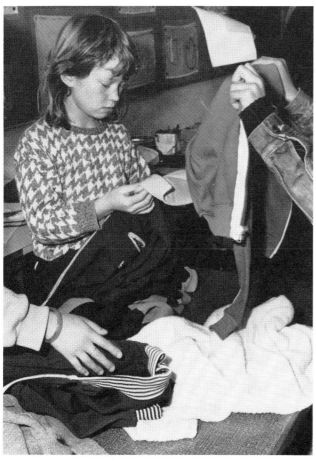

Children sort through old clothes to cut into scraps.

Other children will need to work out exactly what they are going to do first. Let these children make a full-sized rough drawing and then work out which materials they are going to use where. They can cut up the rough drawing to make patterns for the main shapes. Remind them to cut out large shapes first and stick them in place, and then apply smaller details over the top. Some children rush to cut out and stick

down the interesting little details first, then try to fill in round them, which is very difficult and looks messy.

Mixed paper

Get the children to collect sweet-wrappers, wrapping paper, greetings cards, labels, tissue-paper, foil, trays from chocolate boxes, newspapers, etc. They will also need background paper, PVA adhesive for any paper with a shiny or waxed finish, and gum or paste for porous paper.

Follow the methods used in scrap collage and fabric collage to make patterns or pictures.

Tissue-paper

For tissue-paper collages you need to provide white background paper (coloured paper would affect the colour of the tissue-paper by showing through), tissue-paper in a good selection of colours, gum or paste, spreaders, and scissors.

Stress that tissue-paper has a special translucent quality which the children should exploit in their work.

Show them how tissue-paper can be layered to make deeper tones of one colour, and how two or more colours can be overlaid to produce new shades altogether.

When sticking tissue-paper to the background, apply adhesive first and put the tissue on to it, gently smoothing out as many creases as possible. Don't worry if there are creases left, as these will add texture to the picture.

A thin layer of gum can be applied over the finished picture to make the surface slightly shiny and more durable.

Tissue-paper can also be used to create a raised surface. Because it is thin but strong, it can be twisted into 'ropes' and applied to a background. It can also be crumpled into a ball and covered in a smooth piece of tissue-paper, the edges of the covering paper being twisted together and stuck in place. Used with 'ropes' of tissue-paper and areas of flat colour, these 'balls' or 'bosses' create an interesting surface.

Different ways of arranging string.

String

Provide backing card, paints (optional), thick PVA adhesive and spreaders, scissors, and a good selection of strings and threads.

If the children want a coloured background, they should paint the background card and allow it to dry completely before starting the collage. Then divide the background into a grid, and make a pattern in each square using different types of string used in various ways. Apply the adhesive to each square as you come to it, and embed the string in the adhesive.

String can be wound in a spiral, cut into short lengths and arranged in various ways (in parallel lines, alternately horizontal and vertical, in a basket weave pattern), or it could be fluffed out, cut up and scattered over the square, twisted into various shapes within the square, and so on.

Make sure that every child is able to use a wide variety of types of string. Natural fibre string can be dyed to give a variety of colours as well as pattern and texture.

Photomontage

Supply a good selection of colour magazines, black and white photographs from colour magazines (these are better

Colour magazines are cut up to make a photomontage.

48

quality than monotone photographs from newspapers), backing, gum or paste (the cold-water type is adequate for this), spreaders and scissors.

Ask the children to look for pictures on a theme, such as animals, food, bottles, etc, and cut them out. Arrange them to make a pleasing pattern on the page, allowing pictures to overlap. Then stick them down, remembering to stick the ones underneath first. Blank areas can be painted or crayoned.

The children could also collect pictures of things which go together: for example, families (this could include homes and pets as well as people), the seaside or transport. Let them arrange the pictures carefully before sticking them in position.

Encourage the children to arrange the pictures so that they overlap and make big corporate shapes on the page, rather than spreading out individual pictures over the page with lots of space between each one.

Embroidery

Embroidery

INTRODUCTION

Embroidery is the embellishment of a fabric surface. This is usually accomplished by stitching with a variety of threads, but other materials can also be used.

It is one of the most difficult arts. You have to consider line, colour and texture as well as choosing which fabrics and threads to use, what stitches to use and how. Because of this variety, embroidery offers a great richness of experience and interpretation.

Children need to learn how to select the right materials, make their stitch marks, and feel their way through a design. In order to do this, some aspects must be simplified. For example, you could concentrate on one or two stitches at a time, present a rich range of earthy or landscape colours to choose from, look specifically at texture (perhaps

studying bark or barnacled shells), or aim for movement in the sewing by experimenting with different directions and weights of stitches. These are just some ideas.

Before you start

Embroidery, in comparison with other techniques, takes a long time. If you can't do a sample in an evening, it is probably too big a task for a primary age child. But don't give up the idea – adapt it: reduce the size of the work, simplify some steps, use crayons or dyes as a short cut for basic shapes, have several children working together co-operatively, and use a sewing machine where appropriate to save time.

Before you begin, consider the function of the finished piece:

• Will it be a pictorial panel for display on the wall? If so, how are you going to mount it, and is there enough spare fabric round the edge?

• Will the children make it into a bag, waistcoat, cushion etc?

• Is the scale appropriate? Large surfaces need chunky threads.

• Will several small pieces be sewn together for a large panel? If so, how will you join them, do they need a large backing sheet, and how will it be hung?

• What will you do with the half-finished pieces? A lot of work has gone into them, so can they be used in any way, even if they are just mounted as they are?

Above all, an embroidery should be an inspired, well-designed piece of artwork. It has the great advantage that, once you have started the children off, one idea will keep them occupied for quite a long time, and often compulsively. (I have found ten-year-old boys sewing under the desk in other lessons!)

However, it does need some preparation, both in the construction of a design and in the provision of a variety of suitable materials.

From design to first stitch

Design sources

Here are some ideas of things which might provide inspiration. Often a quick sketch or photograph can be sufficient (magazines are a good source). Use techniques like photocopying, tracing and rubbing, as well as drawing.

The natural world offers countless ideas for designs, such as fruit, bark, trees, landscape shapes, grass patterns and leaves. Visit a local pond and examine snails, insects, examples of camouflage, and so on.

Children may be surprised to find a source of inspiration in themselves and each other. They can also look at isolated aspects of themselves, such as hair, feet, shoes, hands, eyes, and so on.

Use embroidery to expand on maths work (tessellations, Islamic art, number patterns such as triangular numbers, shapes, symmetry etc), and topic work.

Design sources are to be found in the man-made world, too. Mechanical objects, such as locks, wheels, gears, engine parts, spanners and cranes, or buildings, including flats, skylines, castles, churches, their own homes and fairytale homes, can inspire very imaginative work. Even food provides some interesting ideas for design.

Try to organise at least a couple of design sessions and involve the children in the choice of subject. The activity must be relevant to the children in interest, content and level. 'Let's make some marble bags' sounds far more exciting than 'Today we are going to do some sewing.'

Transferring the design to fabric

Infants can often work directly on to fabric, either looking at something in front of them, perhaps a snail, or reliving a recent experience, such as seeing giraffes at the zoo.

They can also start by putting colour on the fabric, using fabric crayons, transfer crayons, screen or block printing, and then sewing into the design.

Lower juniors can spray-dye surfaces and trace designs, transferring them using a transfer pencil and hot iron. Older children can also use transfer paints very sensitively. Avoid using pencil as it makes the threads dirty and is difficult to remove.

Once you have the design, make sure the technique is suitable. For example, flat areas of colour need satin stitch or canvas work. Delicate lines lend themselves to some of the straight stitches or free embroidery work. Flat areas of colour with an overlaid structure, such as a butterfly's wing, might be colour printed or put on with felt-tipped pen and finished with straight stitches.

All the following techniques are worth using:
• Fabric crayons: work directly on to the

fabric (natural or synthetic), first sticking the fabric to the desk with sticky tape to stop it moving. 'Fix' the design by pressing a hot iron on to the fabric. Young children can also use felt-tipped pens, but be careful because just a drop of water will make the design 'run'.
• Transfer crayons: crayon the design on to kitchen, photocopying, or tracing paper. Place the crayoned surface face down on the fabric and press with a hot iron to transfer the colour from the paper to the fabric. A second or even third image can be obtained from successive ironings. This technique works best and is more permanent on synthetics, but will work on other fabrics. (Remember the image will be reversed.)
• Transfer paints: the technique is the same as for transfer crayons, but the design is printed on. Beware of blobs! This needs more control, although 'accidental' effects (eg when colours run) can be very successful. You cannot tell from the painting exactly what colour will appear after ironing, so test the colour on a scrap of fabric first if it is important.
• Embroidery transfer pencil: draw the design on to paper and transfer to the fabric with a hot iron. It can be used on tracing

The design is transferred to fabric and stitched.

paper, and so is ideal for tracing designs. Take care sharpening the pencils as they are very crumbly. (Again, remember the image is reversed.)
• Water soluble felt-tipped pen: use this blue felt-tipped pen to draw on fabric. When you apply water to it (gently with a paintbrush) the line disappears. It is an ideal method for lines you don't want to show afterwards. If you are using lawn or calico, place it over a black outline drawing (taped down so that it doesn't move) and the lines will show through clearly enough for the children to draw over them.
• Permanent overhead projector pens: if it doesn't matter about the design lines remaining on the fabric, these are excellent, as they won't run or disappear.

Fabrics to use

• Unbleached calico is very versatile, and comes in lots of different widths.
• Hessian, plain or coloured, is very easy to use (although it rots after about 20 years).
• Non-woven interfacing, medium or heavyweight, is inexpensive, ideal to sew on, and takes colour well.
• Printed or woven patterns on cotton fabric are good if you use the pattern as the basis of your own design.
• Crimplene is easily available, cheap, and takes transfers well, but you need to use very sharp needles to sew it.
• Needlecord and corduroy are useful because the ridges can be used as a guide for working straight stitches. Experiment with turning small shapes round because the effect alters as the direction of the pile changes.
• Binca should only be used if you are sure it is right for the job; otherwise it is too restricting. It is also very old-fashioned.
• Scrim can be used effectively for pulling threads and interlacing.
• Polystyrene tiles provide a rather different but quite successful surface to sew on. You need long needles and fairly thick thread.
• Embroidery canvas is fine for small pieces of work, and ideal for geometric designs (see 'Canvas stitches' on pages 63–66).

Preparing fabrics

You need sharp shears to cut up the fabric. Make sure that they are not used on paper at all, or they will become blunt.

Make sure the fabric does not fray while it is being worked on by putting clear sticky tape or masking tape around the edge; quite young children can do this successfully. A thin line of PVA adhesive also does the job well, but allow it time to dry.

Primary children do not need the fabric stretched in an embroidery loop, but make sure the stitches are not too long.

Threads and needles to use

• Coton perlé is a mercerised cotton with a silky appearance, and is available in a good colour range. Use numbers 3 to 5 crewel needles.
• Soft embroidery cotton is a thickish yarn with a matt finish. Use numbers 3 to 5 crewel needles.
• Coton à broder is a fine yarn with a slight sheen. It needs to be worked more delicately and is ideal for older children. It usually comes in skeins and so it sometimes becomes tangled: this can be prevented by cutting the skein right through at opposite ends, giving you a bundle of threads the right length. Use numbers 5 to 6 crewel needles.
• Tapestry wool is suitable for canvas stitches, but knitting wool is a much cheaper supplement. Use number 18 tapestry needles.
• Carpet thrums can be obtained from some mills and carpet manufacturers. If they are soft wool, they make an excellent substitute for tapestry wool. Coarser synthetic thrums can be used for couching.
• Textured threads will not pull through the fabric, so use them to couch on top.
• A '40' twist cotton/polyester machine thread is useful for tacking, hemming and using on the machine. Proper tacking thread is a cheap substitute, or try your local market. Use number 7 needles (darners are good).

Preparing threads

Make sure the thread is not too long – no more than about 40 cm. You can start most stitches with a knot on the reverse side.

Thread needles for the children the first couple of times, explaining what you are doing, then make them do it themselves. Fix the thread to the needle for infants with a simple overhand knot.

Small scissors should be sharp enough to cut the threads, and it is useful to have a pair of pointed embroidery scissors available for any unpicking that needs to be done (take care with these as they can be dangerous in the hands of children).

Organising the children

Once children get started on a piece of embroidery they do not need constant help, but this is usually essential at the beginning of a piece of work. There are several ways to avoid a queue of 30 children:

• Organise the classroom into groups, with one group starting their embroideries while the other groups do something they can get on with by themselves.
• Ask parents in to help.
• Make children responsible for all stages of the preparation from design, through the transfer of the image, to securing edges. This will act as a filter, as the fast ones will be ready long before some of the others.
• Show a small number of children – perhaps one from each group – what to do, and make them responsible for instructing the others. That way you only have to deal with a few problems.
• Encourage children to sit in groups and discuss what they are doing, only bringing problems to you when no one else can help.

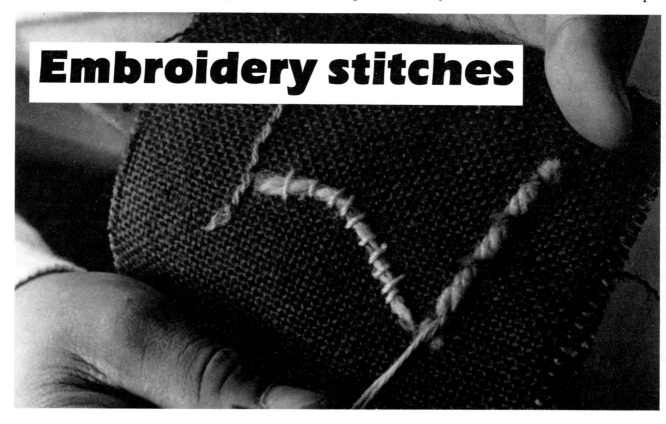

Embroidery stitches

Simple straight stitches

Straight stitches are the simplest and most straightforward, and yet are capable of being used to a high level of sophistication. Many professional embroiderers use only straight stitches.

Once a stitch has been mastered then it can be explored at greater depth – control, careful planning and spacing, use of

56

direction, different thicknesses of thread, different textures, etc.

Never teach more than one or two stitches at a time, but allow these to be thoroughly explored.

Random straight stitches

If children are left to make their own marks on fabric, these are the stitches they will do. Changing the direction of the stitch can be a powerful element in the design.

Satin stitch

When straight stitches are placed close and parallel to each other, they are known as satin stitch. They are particularly good for blocks of colour.

 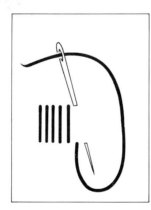

Satin stitch.

Running stitch

Here the needle is threaded in and out of the fabric, leaving a broken line. The gaps between the stitches can be filled in with a further line of stitches, the same colour or

different – this is known as double running stitch.

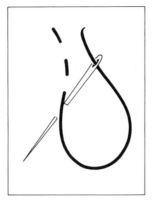 

Running stitch.   Double running stitch.

Back stitch

This is often used for outlining, since it gives the effect of a straight line. Each stitch is made in the opposite direction to the way the line is going. Start with a short straight stitch and bring the needle out of the fabric, the distance of one stitch along. The stitch is completed by taking the needle back down the previous stitch. Bring the needle out ahead again, ready for the next stitch.

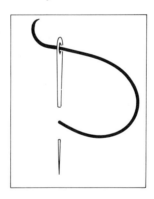

 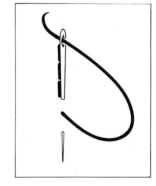

Back stitch.

Any of these stitches can be made more interesting by interlacing them with a contrasting thread once they have been sewn.

The stitches, especially running stitch, can be used in a very free way so that the children are designing with stitches. For example, they may create the movement of ripples on a pond, or the undulations found in a landscape.

Couching for curves and texture

I have put couching before free embroidery stitches because it is essentially a simpler technique.

The aim is to lay a thread on the surface of the fabric and to keep it in place by stitching with another thread. Many of the threads and knitting yarns available today have exciting colours and textures, but cannot be threaded into sewing needles. or pulled through the fabric. The answer is to lay them on top of the fabric and secure them in place with small stitches of a finer thread.

Threads may be tied down with quite different stitches, sometimes almost invisible, and sometimes so that the original thread hardly shows.

A considerable amount of control can be exercised in placing the threads to be couched, and the whole shape can be determined before it is stitched in place.

This technique can be developed to quite a sophisticated level, by using different free embroidery stitches to secure the couched thread, by making loops in it, and by covering whole areas.

Choosing the threads

Any thread can be couched down, including raffia, torn fabric, braids, string, and threads made by the children by knotting other threads together. (This technique can also be used to secure 'found' objects, such as twigs, washers, feathers, strips of fur fabric or shiny paper, bent wire, etc.)

When selecting the thread you will use to sew the first one down, consider whether it is to show or not. Should it be in a matching or contrasting colour? Should it be thick, like coton perlé, or thin for invisibility, like machine cotton? Thread of the same colour as the background is often successful.

Simple couching

Lay the thread to be couched across the surface – either singly or as a bundle of threads – and work small straight stitches at right angles to the thick thread, so that it is secured in place.

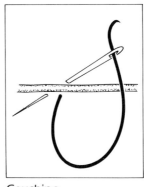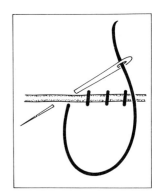

Couching.

Variations

• Vary the spacing between the securing threads: for example, work two stitches then leave a gap.
• Pull the thick thread out in a loop between groups of securing stitches.
• Use other stitches to secure, such as cross stitch, herringbone, chain etc. (see 'Free embroidery stitches' on pages 59–63).
• Have the thick threads crossing in a grid shape and tie them down with stitches where they cross each other.

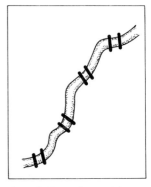

A variation of couching.

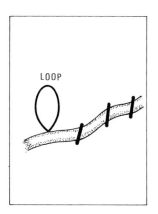

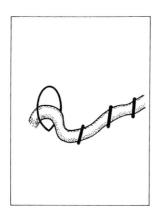

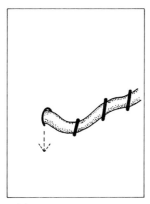

Finishing off couching.

Finishing off

If you do not want the ends of the couched threads to show, they can be pulled through to the back of the work. Push a loop of strong thread through from the back to the right side of the work with a needle, put the end you want to lose through this, and pull the loop back through the fabric, taking the end with it.

Follow-up

Experiment with a variety of both surface and securing threads.

Buy natural-coloured textured threads and dye them randomly or the colours you want.

It is possible to buy tufty knitting yarn, or you may be given some fringing. Dye this with fabric dyes or crayons before couching down. This makes very effective grass etc.

Free embroidery stitches

Traditional decorative stitches can be used to express ideas in design with variety and creativity.

Some of the most useful ones are explained here for you to dip into – certainly not to do all at once. Choose your favourites, or try out a new stitch you haven't used before, to introduce to the children.

Be careful not to use too many different stitches. Often just one or two contrasting ones are enough, such as cretan stitch and French knots, but use each stitch in a variety of ways.

Encourage the children to be imaginative and creative. Try different threads, spacing and sizes of stitch. Work stitches on top of each other. Use fine threads for distance and thicker thread in the foreground to give perspective. Freely placed stitches will give more movement to a design than a row of formally arranged ones.

Eyelet stitch

This is a circular stitch which is useful for mossy banks or stones, barnacles, wheels, etc. Place them close together worked in coton perlé for a jewel-like texture.

Using a point, make a small hole in the fabric (open-weave fabrics, such as hessian,

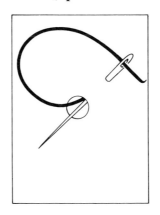

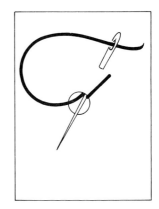

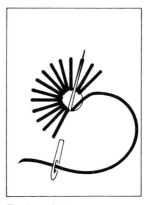

Eyelet stitch.

are good for this stitch). Bring the needle out through the centre hole, insert it at the edge of the eyelet, then bring it up through the centre hole again. At this point, make a sharp tug on the thread. Continue working round in a circular direction until the eyelet is completed. If you want a large hole in the middle of your eyelet, tug hard; if not, tug gently.

Herringbone

This is used for lines and borders, to secure edges and to stop fraying, but it is also decorative in itself.

The row of stitches grows from left to right, but the needle always points in the opposite direction.

Bring the thread out of the fabric, take it diagonally upwards and make a short back stitch. Then take the needle down diagonally and make another back stitch, giving a second row of stitches at the bottom. Continue with an upwards diagonal, and so on.

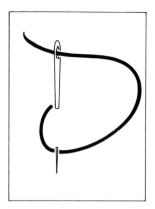
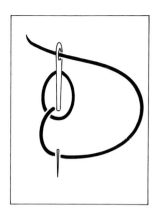

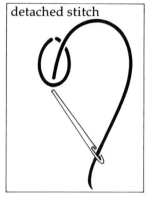

detached stitch

Chain stitch.

Chain stitch

This loop stitch needs a lot of control and is difficult for younger children, but it is good for curly lines, and small circles or ovals. It can also be worked in separate loops – this is called detached chain stitch (sometimes known as lazy daisy).

Draw the needle through the fabric, then insert it back into the same place – the loop formed is secured in place, either by a small stitch (detached chain) or by the beginning of the next stitch.

It is important to prevent the loop from disappearing by placing it just ahead of where the needle will emerge and putting your thumb on the thread to keep it in place.

Fly stitch

Fly stitch is a loop stitch rather like a spread-out chain stitch but easier for children to do. It can either be worked in rows of regular patterns or randomly.

Bring the needle out of the fabric to the left of the stitch, and insert it back into the fabric on the right-hand side, making a diagonal stitch to the centre. Make sure the

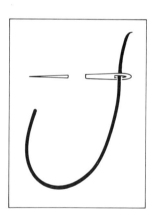
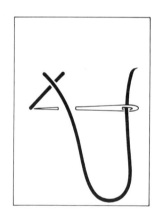

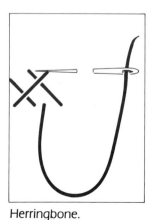

Herringbone.

60

thread loop is caught under the needle, and insert back into the fabric, making a small stitch to secure it.

It is easier if you hold the thread down with the left thumb just ahead of where the needle comes out in the centre.

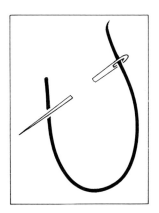

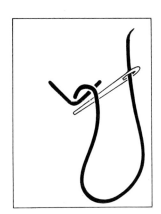
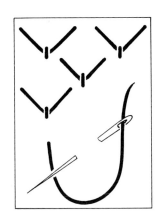

Fly stitch.

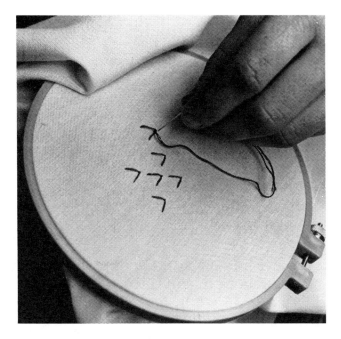

Cretan stitch

This is a useful looped stitch which can be worked close together to make different shapes (eg leaves), or openly in a free way. Again, it is easier than chain stitch.

Make short vertical stitches alternately upwards and downwards, in each case making sure that when the needle comes out of the fabric the thread is caught round it. Each of the small vertical stitches is about one third of the stitch height, but you can vary this for different effects.

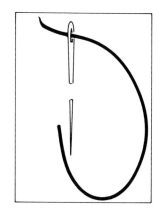
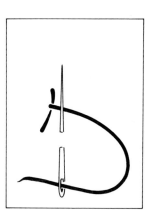

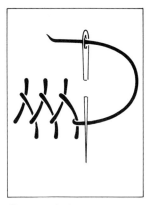

Cretan stitch.

Blanket stitch

This gives the effect of straight stitches with a line along the top. It is useful for landscapes, and can be used to secure hems and in appliqué work. It can be worked in circles and in wavy lines. Used close together it is called buttonhole stitch.

Bring the needle out at the bottom edge

61

of the stitch. Insert the needle above this and slightly to the right, then bring it out next to the original stitch, catching the loop round the needle before pulling it tight.

French knots

These are ideal for dots and can be worked close together for textured effects.

Bring the needle to the right side of the fabric and, holding the thread firmly with the left hand (if you are right-handed), twist it twice round the needle and insert it back through the fabric close to the starting point. Then pull the thread through to the back of the fabric. Put one finger on the knot while the thread is being pulled through to keep it in place.

If French knots are being used for texture, it doesn't matter if they are uneven since this adds to the effect. If you want a dot, such as an eye or a nostril, this is the best stitch to use.

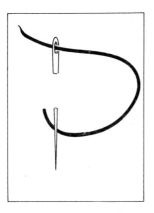

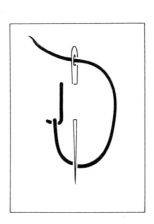

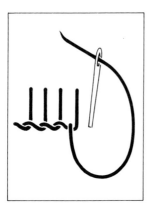

Blanket stitch.

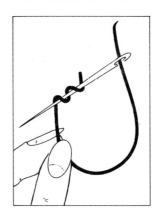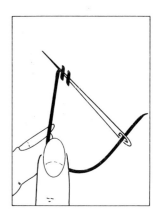

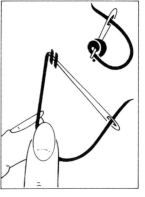

French knots.

Seeding

If you want to shade an area of a design with stitches, short straight stitches can be used – this is called seeding. Make sure that all the stitches go in different directions.

Various tones can be obtained by working stitches in the same thread either close together or scattered.

Seeding.

Follow-up

When each stitch has been mastered in its standard form, try some variations. Overlap them, or extend each stitch sideways to give a rich texture. Vary the thread both in colour and thickness. Try working very fine threads over the same stitch done in a coarser thread.

Get the children to imitate the stitch marks with pen or pencil on paper. This will extend the range of marks available to them when drawing, and is particularly useful for pen-and-ink shading and textures.

Canvas stitches

Embroidery canvas provides an even, structured grid for stitches and is stiff enough for sewing fairly long straight stitches without puckering. It is ideal for geometric designs, without necessarily using complicated stitches. Straight stitches, such as satin stitch, are recommended.

Young children should use a fairly coarse canvas, preferably plastic, and straight stitches. Older juniors could gain a great deal of satisfaction from a detailed design worked in half-cross stitch.

Make sure that the piece of canvas is not too large or the embroidery will take too long to do, and do not necessarily expect all the canvas to be covered.

Canvas is measured by the number of threads to the inch (or 2.5 cm), and ten-hole is the most common. It can be either single mesh (mono) or double mesh (Penelope). The latter is best for half-cross and cross stitch.

It is essential to enclose the canvas edge in masking tape to prevent it from fraying and to stop the threads catching on it.

A design outlined in black and placed under the canvas can be seen clearly through it, and the design lines can be drawn on to the canvas using permanent overhead projector pens.

Unlike other sewing, canvas work is started with a knot in the thread on the right side of the work. Thread the needle through the canvas from the front at a point you will later cover with stitches, about 2.5 cm ahead of the starting point. Then bring the thread through the canvas where you wish to start and commence stitching. The stitches will cover the thread at the back and secure it, so that by the time the knot is reached it can safely be cut off.

This trick is only necessary when starting to sew in a new place. Normally the yarn can be started and finished by threading it under a few stitches at the back of the work.

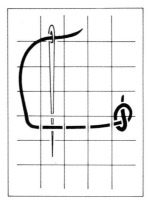

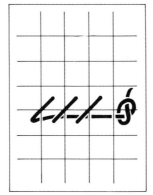

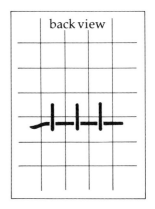

back view

Canvas work.

Half-cross stitch

This stitch gives most detail and is the simplest, after straight stitches. The thread comes out of the canvas and up at an angle of 45° diagonally across to the next hole. It then goes vertically downwards at the back of the canvas into the hole below, ready for the next stitch. The back should consist of a series of short vertical lines.

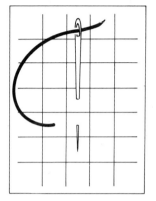  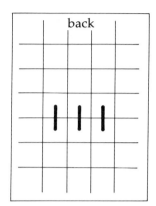

Half cross stitch.

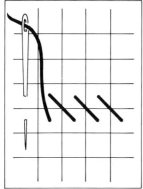 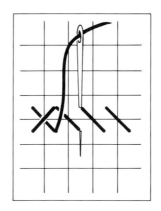 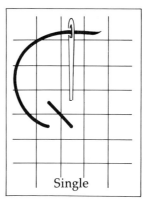

Single

Cross stitch.

Cross stitch

Each stitch consists of a half-cross with another stitch overlapping to make a diagonal cross. Crosses can either be made singly or in rows. In the latter case a row of half stitches is made first and the stitches completed by working top diagonals in the opposite direction.

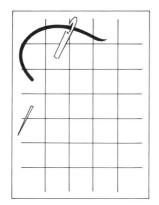 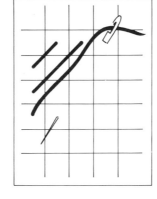 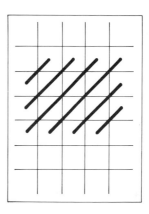

Cushion stitch.

Cushion stitch

Cushion stitch makes use of the diagonal across the grid, small stitches being made from edge to edge to complete a square. The basic square can be of almost any size, from two holes by two holes (properly called mosaic stitch) up to about seven by seven.

Interesting effects are obtained by grouping stitches with the threads going in different directions, or by alternating with squares of half-cross stitch.

  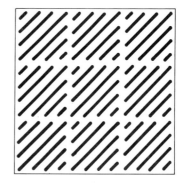

Different ways of using cushion stitch.

Follow-up

There are many other canvas stitches which can be found in any book on canvas embroidery, but make sure they are used to good effect and not just as a routine exercise.

To try out different stitches with older children, first choose a design such as a landscape with fields, then each field can be sewn in a different stitch. Other ideas for the basis of a 'modern sampler' like this are tessellations and cityscapes.

Displaying and making things

Displaying the embroideries

Remember that the designs can be mounted and displayed by themselves and also alongside the completed work.

Designs and/or embroideries can be photocopied and worked into with pencil or

pen as the basis for further design.

For mounting and blocking you will need some stiff card to stretch them over, strong thread and a needle for lacing or masking tape to stick the fabric to the board, some pins, soft board (such as a pinboard or plywood) for blocking, old sheeting or white blotting paper, staples or drawing-pins, and clean water in a spray.

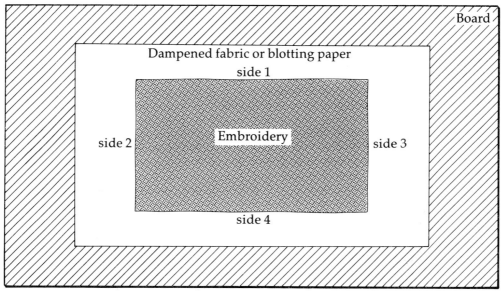

Blocking of finished embroidery.

Ideally, the board should first be covered with damp cloth, such as old sheeting, or white blotting paper, stapled or pinned in place. Canvas embroidery is blocked face downwards (you can then add extra water to the back), and other types face up.

Place the embroidery on the board, gently spray with the water and pin it along one side. Then pin the side at right angles to this, pulling the embroidery back into a square or rectangular shape. Next pin the side opposite that and finally the side parallel to the first one you did, each time pulling the fabric back into shape.

Allow the work to dry for at least a day and remove it from the board.

The embroidery is now stretched over the piece of card which has been cut to a suitable size, smaller than the fabric.

To make sure that the embroidery is evenly stretched put pins around the edge of the cardboard, working from the centre of each side outwards.

Now turn the loose fabric over on to the back of the card and secure it. Ideally, this is done by lacing with a strong thread which is pulled tight before being fastened off. But you could stick it down with masking tape instead. The pins are then removed.

The embroidery can then be displayed on the wall as it is, or a mount can be cut to fit in the usual way.

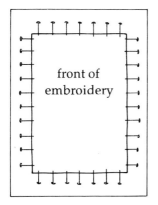
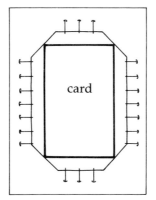
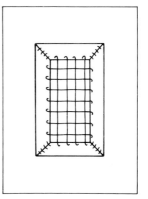

Stretching an embroidery over card.

Making things

Using a sewing machine

As machining can take some time, it is best to keep the machine going during other lessons, with only two children using it at the same time. Show one child how to use the machine with another watching, and then get them to swap places. Once they are used to the machine they can help each other and point out pitfalls. All you need to do is fill the bobbin when it runs out.

Most things are sewn right sides together, and corners are clipped (cut off along the diagonal) so that the corners are neat when turned right side out.

Cushions

Embroider the front of the cushion and cut the back out of matching or contrasting fabric of the same size.

The best stuffing consists of foam chips, since these are washable, but the children may be able to bring in their own fillings. Ideally, enclose the filling in a bag 5 cm larger than the cushion (use old sheeting with the cushion front as a pattern).

To construct the cushion, pin and tack the front and back right sides together and machine round the edge, leaving a gap large enough to insert the filling. Stuff the cushion (this is best done outside), then turn in the edges on the opening and pin them together. Oversew the opening closed.

Drawstring bags

Embroider one side of the bag, then cut a second side the same size as the first. Pin and tack the two pieces, right sides together, along three edges, leaving the top open. Sew by machine and clip the bottom corners. Turn over the top edge and sew round to make a casing for the drawstring.

Turn the bag right side out, and make a small hole in the casing on each side where the seam is. Cut two pieces of string, each twice the width of the bag plus 10 cm. Thread each piece (one from each side) all the way round and tie the ends together with an overhand knot. Pull both loops to close the bag.

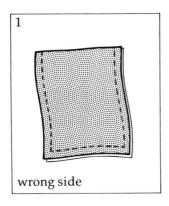

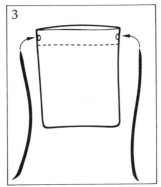

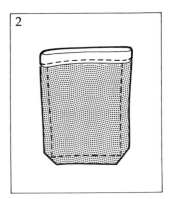

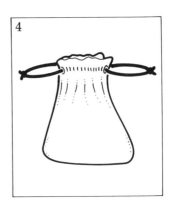

The stages in making a drawstring bag.

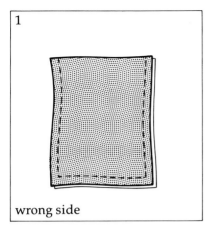

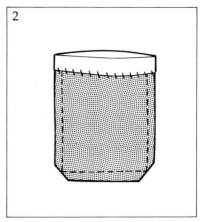

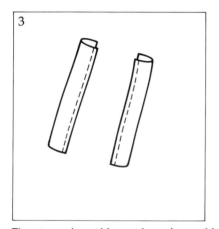

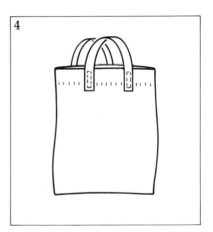

The stages in making a shopping or kit bag.

Shopping/kit bags

These have handles made from a piece of matching fabric folded over and machined together. The handles can be made long to wear over the shoulder (measure them on the child) or short.

Embroider one or both sides of the bag. Join the two sides together as for the drawstring bag and hem the top by machine. Sew the handles to each side in a loop.

Waistcoats

Buy one pattern, the simpler the better, to fit one of the larger children in the class. Cut the pattern out in non-woven interfacing and transfer all the markings on to it with a pencil. Pin this pattern on to each child in turn, making larger seams where necessary.

Take the pattern off the child, mark with extra pins where the pattern was pinned together, and use this to cut out the fabric. Older children can cut out their own paper patterns from the pinned one.

Embroider the waistcoat as required, sew the shoulder and side seams together, then bind the edges or make a simple hem. Denim, bought cheaply at a local market, is an ideal fabric for this.

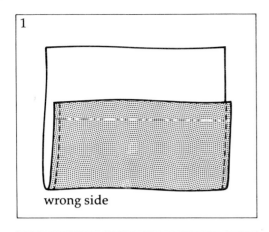

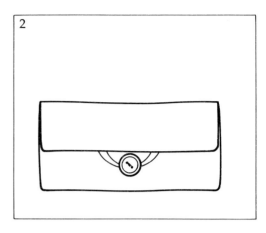

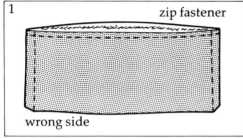

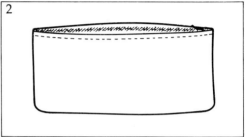

The stages in making a pencil case or purse.

Pencil cases/purses

Start off with a large rectangle of material. If the case or purse is designed with a flap, make sure the flap is slightly shorter than the other two pieces, and that the embroidery is suitably placed and not covered up. Sew up the two sides, right sides together, and attach a button and a loop for fastening.

Alternatively, use a zip fastener the same length as the rectangle. First sew each long side to one side of the zip, then turn it inside out and sew the sides together. Open the zip (from the inside) and turn it back to the right side.

Follow-up

Get the children to design embroideries for specific purposes (not necessarily to be made up) after they have had some experience with stitches. For example, design the front of a space jacket, a treasure bag, a panel for the headteacher's study, a cushion for themselves, an elaborate saddle, a book cover for their favourite book and so on.

Embroideries which have been mounted and displayed on the wall can be sewn on to the middle of a favourite cushion or a pocket, attached to a bought pencil case, and so on.

Tiny embroidered cushions could be filled with lavender or pot pourri.

Clay

Clay

INTRODUCTION

Clay work is fun! Every child can achieve a product which is uniquely theirs, especially once they understand that being original is being creative. They should be persuaded to amend and alter their design to achieve the results they want.

It is also important to persuade them that creating and working with the hands is worthwhile and personally fulfilling, and not merely an activity done in school only when 'work' is completed.

Pottery is not just an art form, where people derive great satisfaction from producing aesthetically pleasing work. It has always been a great source of industrial wealth for many nations. Think of Doulton, Royal Worcester, Wedgwood, Ainsley, Poole and many others, without which we would be a poorer nation.

Pottery helped mankind to survive over centuries, being used for storing food and drink. It is a world resource which is used not only for pots but as bricks for houses, tiles for bathrooms, sparking plugs for cars, just to mention a few.

The aims of clay work

The main objective of working in clay is to develop the skill of design, manipulative powers and an awareness of the beauty which can be achieved in pottery.

At every stage of development and in every article made, the children should design within a given set of rules and with given tools.

Manipulative skills are always being extended, as each step from thumb pots to coil pots adds another process for the hands and minds to understand and master.

The use of colour, whether in glaze or paint, provides continual practice in colour harmony, and develops aesthetic awareness.

It is important that children are educated to use their senses so that, as they grow, they will be able to make sound balanced judgements about all art forms and about the artefacts with which they will inevitably surround themselves.

Long-lasting and useful models are more worth while than rockets and moon surfaces made out of egg-boxes. This is perfectly adequate for five- to seven-year olds, but after that children are capable of more sophisticated craft skills and a greater sense of achievement.

Hopefully the approach taken in this chapter will encourage children to see the pleasure and advantages of being truly creative in a practical way.

Getting ready to start

• Always attempt any pottery task yourself before taking a lesson.
• Make sure that every child has all the equipment needed to complete a task without having to queue or wait for someone else to finish using a tool; it's very frustrating for a child who has a brilliant idea to be unable to proceed with it.

• Find out how many children will be participating in each lesson throughout the year. Analyse the procedures and equipment required for each lesson, and have an organised plan for getting the equipment out well in advance.
• Make it clear to the children how you expect them to behave. For example, keeping their hands and the clay over the table at all times avoids spillage on to the floor and dirt spreading throughout the school. It also helps the cleaners and lowers the health hazard from clay dust.
• Don't worry about pottery wheels. A small piece of chipboard approximately 18 cm square which the children can turn around will do very well indeed. Do not use ordinary timber board as the clay will stick to it, whereas chipboard is porous and releases the clay. You will need larger pieces of chipboard when rolling larger areas of clay, in the region of 40 cm by 60 cm.
• Hardwood pottery tools for a class of 30 can be expensive, so buy a piece of 5 mm

Pastry cutters are useful for slab pottery.

dowel rod, cut it into pencil-sized pieces and slope one end down. These make ideal tools. Old pastry cutters can be used for tile or slab pottery, since good tile cutters can be rather expensive. Broom handles and broken rounders bats make excellent rolling pins for slab work. Old screws, keys, blunt knives, pins, round-ended scissors, ancient pen nibs and lino cutters make excellent indenting tools.

• A few water jars and some 1 cm wide paintbrushes are useful, as are an assortment of paintbrushes for glazing or painting, buckets for storing clay, and freezer bags for storing work in progress.

• When the pottery has been biscuit fired, there are several ways of decorating it. Glazing is the obvious choice, but PVA-based paints and balsa paint work well, making the children's work bright and attractive. You will therefore need a variety of clear glazes and dyes or coloured glazes which have to be mixed in advance of any glazing session. This of course depends on the clay you have used and the firing temperature of your kiln.

• For the paints you will needs lots of mixing jars and brushes. These must be washed well or they harden up quickly and have to be thrown away, which can be very expensive.

Display

There are many ways to display finished articles. They can be wall-mounted on timber or stood on polished wooden blocks (off-cuts can often be obtained from timber merchants very cheaply).

Alternatively, the children could make their own wooden ornament shelf.

Knives, screws, keys, pins and many other objects could be used to make designs on pottery.

Thumb pots

The simple thumb pot

As in most learning situations, one skill at a time needs to be taught. Once the children have made and decorated one or two balanced and well-designed pots, they can add pieces of clay to it to make the 'Thumb pot candle holder' (see page 79). But don't try both processes at once – it may well lead to disaster, and a 45-minute lesson goes very quickly when trying a new skill!

The simple thumb pot is about right for nine- to ten-year-olds to start with,

persevering until they achieve satisfactory results.

You will need to provide the following materials: a small piece of chipboard (approximately 150 mm square), small wooden pottery tools or 5 mm diameter dowel rod strips with an angled point, a ball of clay approximately 5 cm in diameter, stoneware clay, screws, nails, pins, keys, pastry cutters and any serrated edged tool which makes an interesting pattern.

Always make sure the children wear overalls.

Pick up the clay and roll it gently into a small ball. Cup the hand which you don't

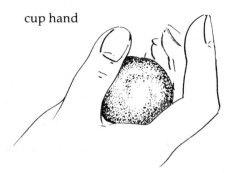

cup hand

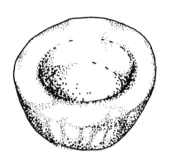

usually write with and sit the ball in it. (Don't put the clay down on to the board until the basic pot shape has been made.)

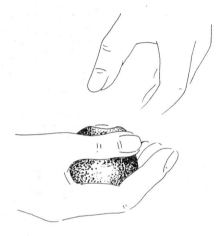

With the thumb of the other hand, make a small dent into the centre top of the

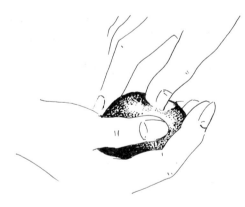

ball of clay, by squeezing gently and evenly on to the outside of the ball. At the same time, revolve the ball with the thumb and fingers inside the 'cup hand', as if you are screwing a large bottle top on carefully.

Ensure that the squeezing thumb works constantly downwards, at the same time pushing outwards. Otherwise very thin

78

With correct pressure actions, the pot should be about 0.5 cm or 1 cm thick. Finger prints can be smoothed off by gentle finger pressure on the bumps.

Now, using both hands, hold your pot up to your own eye level, and turn it round slowly, gently easing the clay into a smooth symmetrical shape.

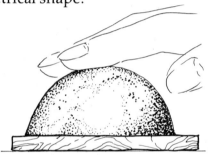

Place the pot upside down on the chipboard and give it a gentle tap. This helps to give it a level top edge. Then, using the tips of your fingers, smooth out any bumps.

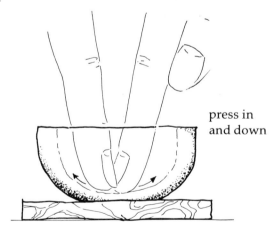

press in and down

Turn it the correct way up on the board, and gently press with the tips of the fingers down into the bottom of the pot to give it an even flat base.

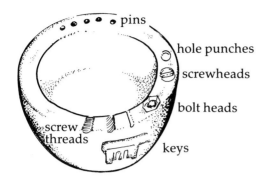

pins

hole punches

screwheads

bolt heads

screw threads

keys

Now interesting patterns can be impressed into the pot using a variety of tools.

Leave the thumb pots to dry out for three to seven days before firing, depending on the atmosphere of your workshop. The temperature of the kiln fire ideally should be about 1100°C.

Using a variety of coloured glazes the children can experiment with colour. Don't use sophisticated adult colour tones; mix colour stains with ordinary clear glaze which can then be remixed in yoghurt pots to give a wide variety of shades.

Make a bucket of clear glaze, which should have the consistency of thin cream. Allow the children to dip their own pots in. This can be messy, so provide plenty of clean water, rags and paper towels. Dip the pots for two or three seconds only, or the porous biscuit-fired pots will reject the liquid, just like a soaked sponge.

Have plenty of good brushes available.

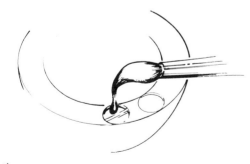

drip action

The additional colour glaze should be applied by using the brush as a 'drip tool', because the glaze dries extremely quickly and a normal painting action does not work very well. It calls for a very careful and patient action, by allowing the glaze to drip from the brush bristles on to the place which needs the colour.

If you find it difficult to organise the glazing procedure, the children could paint the pots instead, with Balsa paints or PVA colour paints.

French white polish can be applied when the paint is perfectly dry. This is easier to manage than clear varnish, as it dries very quickly, but it is rather more expensive.

Thumb-pot candle holders

A *simple thumb-pot candle holder with legs and a head.*

Start off by making a fairly substantial thumb pot.

Choose a candle to be fitted into the base of the thumb pot, and press it gently

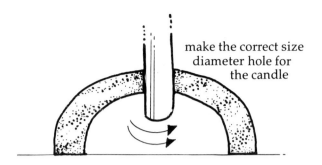

make the correct size diameter hole for the candle

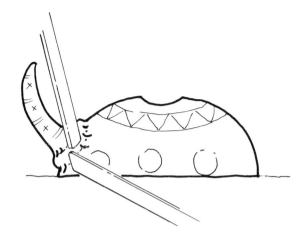

down and round into the bottom base of the upturned pot.

disappears. Ensure that the children do this well, otherwise the parts drop off when the clay dries.

Biscuit fire the pots as usual, and glaze or paint as preferred. Ensure that the bottom of the pot is wiped clean from any glaze, otherwise it will stick to the kiln floor. Make sure that the pots have really cooled down before removing them from the kiln, to prevent fine cracking.

Christmas candle holder

Place the holder on a very stiff piece of cardboard or plywood rectangles 1.5 cm thick.

Stick pine cones, sprigs of holly, etc, and perhaps a small ribbon bow on to the rectangles, and the Christmas candle holder is complete. These make attractive table decorations for Christmas.

Decorate the upturned thumb pot by adding interesting shapes and pieces to the outside, such as a head, legs and eyes, leaves and flowers, handles etc.

Join the pieces to the pot by rolling out pieces of clay as thick as a piece of string, using this as a joining agent between the two parts.

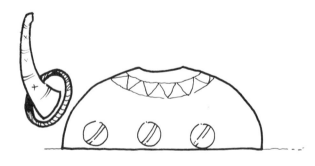

For example, to attach a tail, wrap a coil of clay around, like a collar, on to the tail and place both against the side of the pot. With the pottery tool, work the clay collar evenly in a smooth pressing motion against the pot and the tail at the same time. Smooth it down evenly so that the join seam

Clay eggs

Clay eggs normally take between 45 minutes and one hour to make after demonstration. You will need to provide clay, pottery tools, chipboard, knives, cardboard, pencils and brushes.

Get the children to make two thumb pots, larger than usual. Make sure that the thickness is even and each pot is similar in size.

Tap the edges flat and level, then place the edges of the two pots together and join them with a piece of thinly coiled clay. It helps to dampen the edges slightly, and score them with a pottery tool.

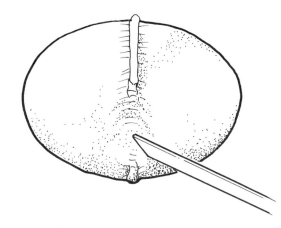

Smooth out the joining clay so that no seam lines are visible, and make the egg as smooth as possible with the fingers. Sometimes, a slightly damp paintbrush can help to smooth the egg beautifully. Preserve it in a freezer bag.

hole to avoid explosion

The children could design their eggs on card first. Ask them to draw on hands, feet,

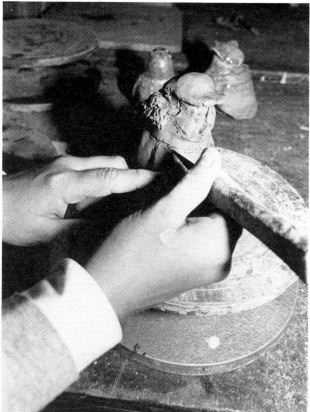

A clay egg develops a character as features are added.

hats, legs, faces, clothes, and so on. These can then be made from clay and added on to the surface of the clay egg. Remember to use the thinly coiled clay as a joining agent.

Indented patterns should also be encouraged to give the children practice in textured surfaces.

hole to avoid explosion

Always make a hole somewhere in the egg to avoid an explosion.

Once the egg creatures have been made and fired, they can be glazed or painted, then mounted on polished blocks of timber for display.

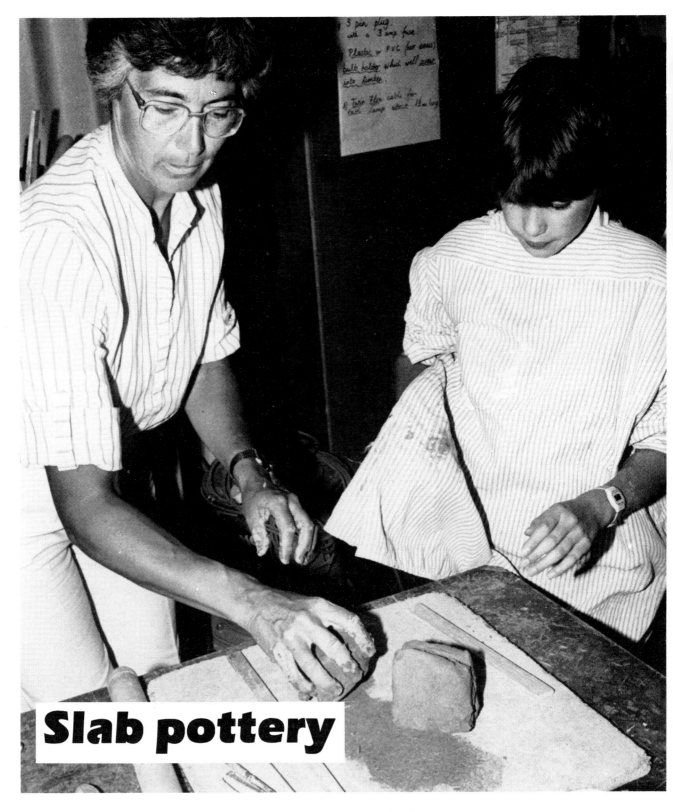

Slab pottery

Flat masks

As the children progress through working with clay they always want something new to do; this simple face mask helps them to get used to a new technique – rolling out clay with a rolling-pin to get it into an even

flat thickness.

The children will need card, pencils, crayons, slats of wood, rolling-pins, clay, chipboard, 9 mm dowel rods, paints, varnish, adhesive and cutting tools.

Draw an interesting monster face on card, or discuss masked balls where people

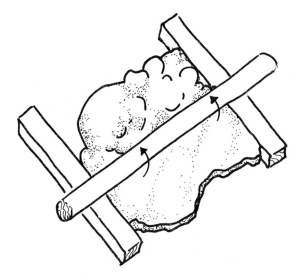

rod handle. Make a small rectangle of flat clay to fit over the dowel rod on the back of the mask. Attach the clay rectangle and roll the dowel rod inside the rectangle and against the mask. Then withdraw the dowel rod, leaving a clay casing into which the dowel rod will fit after the clay has been fired.

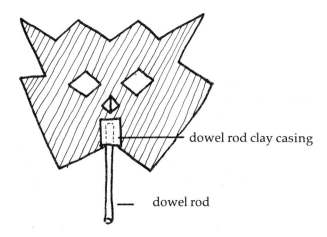

dress up in fancy dress. (This can also be a starting point for drama lessons.)

When the children's own designs have been drawn and coloured, proceed to rolling the clay out. Take two slats of wood (about 2 cm wide and 3–4 mm thick), and place a piece of clay (about the size of a tennis ball) in between the two pieces of wood and on a large piece of chipboard.

Using a rolling-pin or an old broom handle cut down, keep the ends of the rolling-pin on the slats of wood and roll the clay flat. This ensures an even thickness of clay.

When the flat slab of clay has been rolled out, the designs can be cut out and pieces added to it to make a dramatic effect.

After firing the mask, paint and varnish it. A dramatic effect can be achieved with paints.

Finally insert the dowel rod handle and secure it with PVA adhesive.

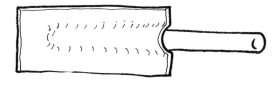

If the plaque is to be used as a mask, turn it over to make a fixing for the dowel

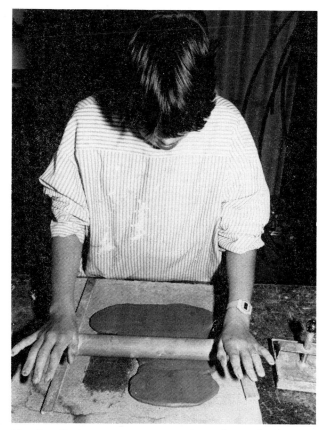

Clay is rolled out between two slats of wood.

Tile design task

This activity, for older juniors, requires an organised, forward-planning mind, as children learn to follow a design task which has been externally set through to the finish. It introduces accurate design drawing and using the balance of line, design and colouring.

You will need a hexagonal tile cutter, hole-saws, card, paper, pencils, pairs of compasses, colours, clay, rolling-pins, slats of wood, knives, timber, a tri-square, saws, sanding paper and PVA adhesive.

Arrange five hexagons in a tessellation on which either straight lines or circles have been drawn. There can be two straight lines and two circles, two straight lines and one circle, or two circles and one straight line.

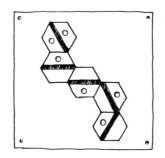
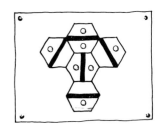

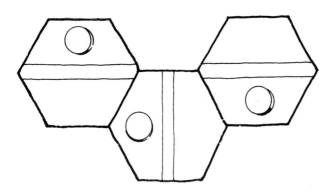

The lines and circles can be placed anywhere on the tile as long as the straight lines reach from one edge of the tile to the other. In clay, the straight lines will have to be narrow strips and the circles cut out and mounted on to the tile.

When the design has been drawn and coloured, roll the clay out using the slab pottery method decribed in 'Flat masks' (page 82).

Cut out the tiles using the hexagonal tile cutter, and place strips and circles of clay in position. (Use pastry cutters or hole-saws for the circles.) These must be very carefully joined using the thin coil method. Pottery tools and knives must be used delicately to achieve a smooth, accurate design.

While the tiles are drying out, place the chipboard on top of them to keep them flat. Fire the hexagons after they have dried out,

and glaze them very carefully. The designs must show clearly which glaze colours are to be used.

Choose a suitably shaped piece of redwood for mounting the tiles. Sand and polish the timber, then fix the tiles in position using PVA adhesive.

Drill screw holes into the corners of the timber to make an attractive wall mounting.

Table lamps

The idea behind making slab pottery into a table lamp was to introduce children to the idea that technology is there to be used, and that various materials can be used in harmony to create a worthwhile article.

This is more suitable for 11- to 12-year-olds. It needs great care and concentration, and can only be achieved after handling clay regularly. Also the strength needed to roll out the clay and to cut accurately is usually only achieved at this age.

The fired bases have to be glazed carefully. Once refired, the additional parts, such as the timber chiselled blocks, have to be added and the electrical wiring connected. As children get older, they become much more physically and mentally skilful, although at first they find the wiring, mounting and fixing difficult. However, they usually rise to the challenge and are highly delighted when the lamps light up at the testing stage.

You will need some chipboard 4 mm thick, clay, a square tile cutter, pottery tools, scrap items for pattern making, glaze, PVA paint, redwood battens 75 mm × 75 mm, a craft knife, a wood gauge or a pencil and ruler, a tri-square, a tenon saw, a 6 mm chisel, a file, glasspaper, a power drill, an electric sander, French polish, electric flex, a three-pin plug, a 40-watt light bulb, wood adhesive and a lampshade.

The pottery base

Roll out the clay between pieces of wood 4 mm thick as described on page 82. Cut out three squares of clay with a tile cutter. Keep one square for the top and cut the other two in half to make four rectangles for the sides of the lamp.

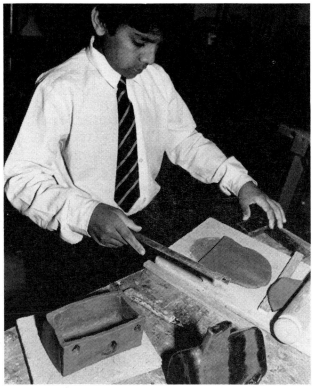

Rolled out clay is cut to the correct size.

Cut out a hole 8 mm in diameter from the centre of the square top for inserting the electric flex.

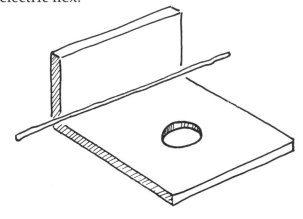

Use coils of clay to stick shapes on to the sides of the lamp, then join the sides together and add the top, again using the coil clay method. Scrape the surface gently with a pottery tool to remove the seam marks and to make the surface smooth.

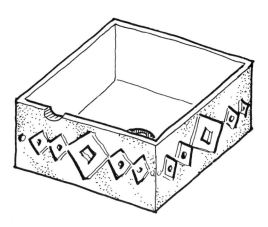

Turn the base upside down and cut away a small, curved piece of clay from the bottom edge on one side of the lamp for the flex.

Then turn it the right way up and use screws, bolts, keys and pins to make interesting designs on the top.

Decorate the base by indenting and adding shapes.

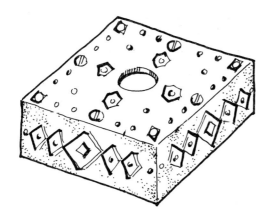

Store the lamps upside down so that the top surface remains flat. Allow them to dry out for five to seven days, then fire them, and finish off with glaze or PVA paint.

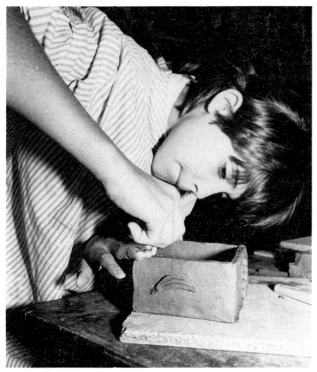

The base is fitted together using the coil clay method.

The wooden lamp fitting

Use a tri-square and a pencil to mark an accurate 10 cm length on the redwood batten, then cut the section with a tenon saw.

Ask the children to design simple patterns to carve into the wooden block consisting of 7 mm lines (1 mm wider than the chisel). Then mark out the patterns on the block with a craft knife.

Use a wood gauge or a pencil and ruler

to mark a 5 mm depth at each corner of the wood, top and bottom. Saw through to the marked depth, then use a chisel to remove thin layers of wood along the lines to the marked depth. Smooth down each groove with a file or glasspaper.

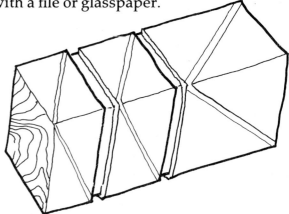

Measure and mark the centre point at each short end of the block, then fix it securely in a clamp. Drill from each end to the centre of the block.

Polish the end-grain with a sander, and French polish the carved block to finish.

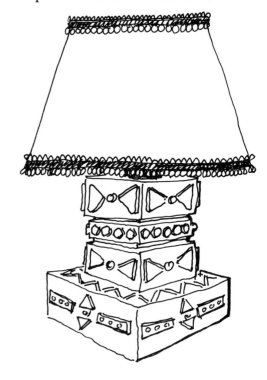

Finishing off

Assemble and wire up the fittings, test the assembly by using an ordinary 40-watt bulb, and stick the wood block to the top of the clay base with wood adhesive.

Coil pottery

Making coil pots

As this is an advanced skill, older children find it easier. It is a new procedure but incorporates the joining techniques used in slab pottery.

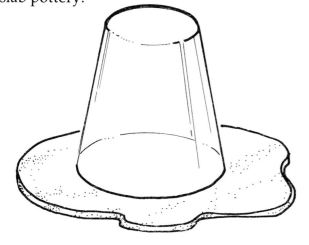

Children will need accurate hand and eye co-ordination. Each coil has to be quite

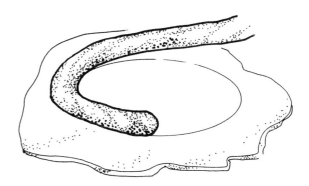

Place on the inside edge of the circle.

cylindrical, so they should practise this.

You need to provide clay, rolling-pins, slats of wood, a circle printer (such as a drinking glass), pottery knives, pottery

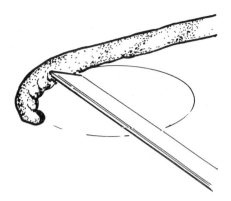

The joining method for coil pottery.

tools, indenting tools, pastry cutters, and large and small pieces of chipboard.

Roll out a piece of clay big enough to indent a circle shape from the top of an ordinary drinking glass, and leave it on the chipboard.

Roll out cylinders of clay about the thickness of a forefinger and join them together. Place the coil carefully on the inside edge of the printed circle.

Always join the ends of a coil at a slant and work the clay across the join with a pottery tool. When the coils are joined to one another, make sure the cut is at a

different place on the circumference of each coil to avoid a dip in the same place every time. Eventually the coils level up.

Using a pottery tool and pressing down on the sloped end of the tool, press into the inside of the coil about half way up and then down into the base, locking the coil into the base. Keep the indentations right next to each other to avoid any holes appearing.

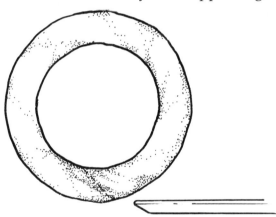

Join at a slant and work the clay across the join.

Place several coils on top of each other, joining each one carefully to the one below it in the same way.

Press in and down.

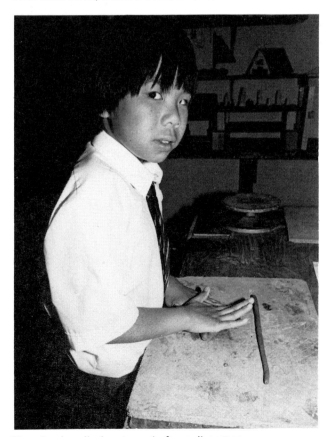

The clay is rolled out ready for coil pottery.

To shape the pot, each coil needs to be slightly smaller or larger in diameter than the last one. This will enable the shape of the pot to move inwards or outwards.

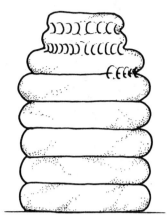

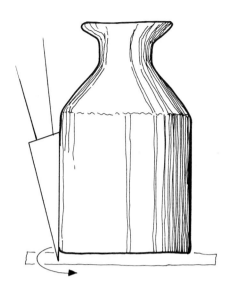

The joining method can now be done on the outside. Then gently tap the top with a piece of chipboard to level off the pot.

To make a textured finish, use the pottery tool to scrape each coil gently on the outside in a vertical motion, eliminating the coil cylinder shape.

Place the pot and base on a pottery wheel. Then use a long sloped pottery knife blade to cut the base shape by holding the nose of the blade by the side of the pot, pressing into the wheel and turning it slowly to cut a sloped base edge.

Add handles and pouring edges, and create texturing with the pottery tools or screws, bolts, nails etc.

When the pots have been fired, glazing should be done by dipping and pouring. Remember to wipe the base clean from glaze.

This pot was shaped by decreasing the coil diameter.

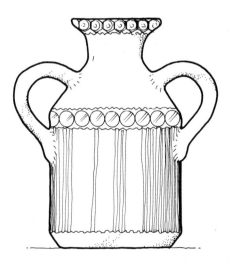

89

Making faces

Mounted faces

After working through the thumb pot stage and coiling, children are eager to attempt more advanced work, making all sorts of creatures and, of course, people.

It is interesting that we all have to learn about the proportion of our own head shapes – how the eyes are set in and the eyebrows are set out, how the bone structure determines the shape of the head, how jaw lines vary, how noses are set in relation to the eyes, the width of the eyes

and the cheek bone setting, how the ears are shaped and where they are in relation to the mouth and nose, how lip shapes vary etc. This is a challenging project and can be attempted first of all by experimenting in Plasticine.

Plasticine trial head

You will need Plasticine, chipboard, clay, pottery tools, knives, tools for making features, glaze or paints and varnish, plywood, a drill and PVA adhesive.

90

Get the children to feel their own faces with their eyes shut – the ins and outs, the dents and bumps.

Then tell them to look in a mirror. How far apart are your eyes? Where is your nose? Does your chin stick out a lot? Is your face round, square, oval? How far back does the side of your face go? Do you have thick or thin eyebrows? How are your ears set?

Using a thumb and finger, they can measure their forehead, the length of their nose, their mouth and chin length. What do they discover?

Discuss proportion, carving out, building up and shape. What does the head look like from a different angle?

With a round ball of Plasticine and a craft knife, cut out the basic head shape, looking at it from all angles. Build up the features with pieces of Plasticine and carve them out with a knife and pottery tool.

When the child is satisfied that they have made a good quality head, the skills and perceptions learned can be transferred

to clay, which is a more difficult substance to work with.

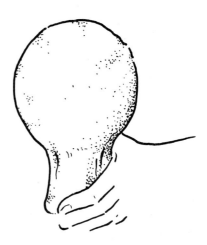

Moving on to clay

Make a ball of clay, just smaller than a tennis ball. Squeeze a neck from the bottom of the

A lump of clay is carefully cut and moulded to match a Plasticine trial head.

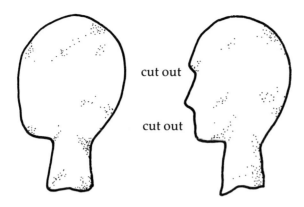

cut out

cut out

ball and mould the basic head shape at the back down to the neck.

Following the Plasticine trial head, carefully cut the basic shape using a knife,

making sure it is correct from all angles.

Now cut back or mould the cheekbone structure.

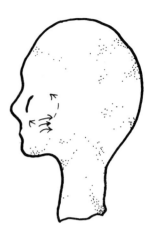

When the nose has been shaped at the front and side and the lips mounted on and into the chin area, begin work on the eyebrows. These can be mounted on with a thin string coil of clay.

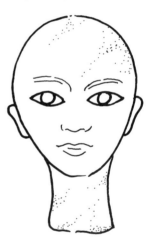

With a pottery tool, cut out oval or almond-shaped holes for the eye sockets. Slightly lift up the edges of the hole. Insert minute rolled balls of clay for the eyeballs, and press gently with a pottery tool so that they don't fall out.

The ears can be cut out of thinly rolled out flat clay, and joined on in the usual way.

When every part has been moulded on to the head, hollow it out before it is fired in the kiln or it may explode.

When the faces have been fired, they can either be glazed or painted and varnished.

A clay eyeball is inserted into the eye socket.

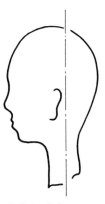

Cut carefully down behind the ears.
Hollow out the back.

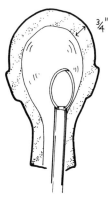

Scrape out with a pottery scraper or a bent piece of metal.
It should look like the inside of a thumb pot.

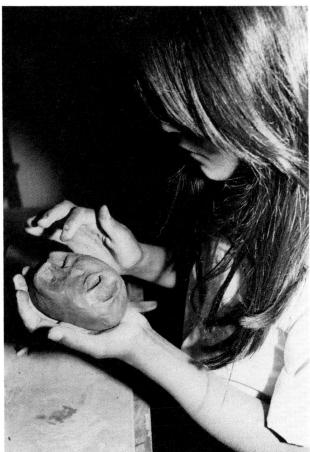

Working on a clay face.

Put PVA adhesive on the edges of the faces and place them on to the plywood rectangles. When they have dried hard, another coat of varnish can be added to the plywood and faces to finish them off.

Cut out rectangles of 1.5 cm thick plywood as a wall plaque, and drill holes in each corner for mounting.

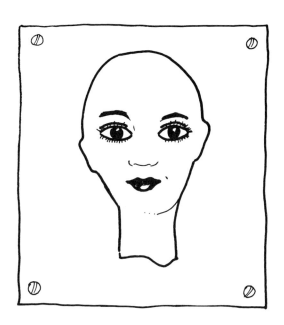

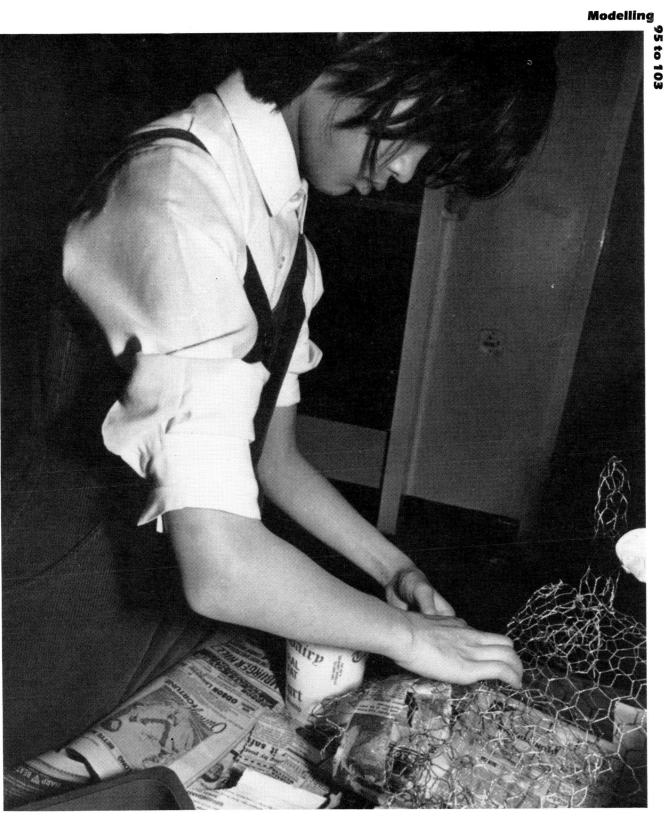

Modelling

Modelling

INTRODUCTION

Making 3D models plays a very important part in the school curriculum right from nursery years. Long before children are thinking about reading, writing or counting they are sticking boxes together and making them into 'things', offering a link between play with provided equipment and making something of their own.

Models provide a great deal of scope for imaginative work. Children have to consider not only the question of shape and substance but also colour, line and texture. They also provide an alternative means of recording information. After all, in making a model of, say, a wasp, careful study is required. How many legs has it? What is the shape of the body? What about the position of the antennae etc? Sometimes children are better motivated to find out for themselves in this way.

There are also other aspects of learning in model-making that should not be overlooked. Many problem-solving situations present themselves – how do particular shapes best fit together and, later on, how will the model work? What kinds of adhesive are best for particular purposes? It is important that the children raise the questions and think out the answers for themselves. Children should be helped to work out their own ideas through discussion, making them more confident and eventually more independent in the process.

It would of course be unrealistic to expect a four-year-old to be able to make a specific model without any adult input, but a great deal is lost if the activity is entirely adult-directed with little or no element of choice.

Starting points

Young children should be given the opportunity to handle a wide variety of materials: waste materials (egg-boxes, newspaper, discarded boxes, cartons and pots made from plastic and card); natural materials (shells, twigs, wood, pine cones,

feathers etc) and Plasticine are all very suitable for working with four-, five- and six-year-olds. They also need access to fabrics, buttons, beads, threads, wools, straws, different kinds of paper etc to use as accessories to their work.

The materials need to be organised efficiently if children are to become independent workers. It is useful to store items in large labelled boxes – one for cardboard containers, another for plastic containers, a third for cardboard rolls and so on. Smaller items can be sorted into labelled trays or ice-cream containers. The children also need to know where to find scissors, glue spatulas and brushes and should be expected to return everything to its place when they have finished.

Model-making has much more potential than slapping a couple of boxes together in the name of creativity when the 'serious work' of the school day has been completed. It should be regarded as a purposeful activity in its own right. Once they have gained a little basic experience in sticking and cutting and are encouraged to think out their work through discussion, children will want to develop their techniques.

Modelling materials ideally should be stored in large, clearly labelled containers.

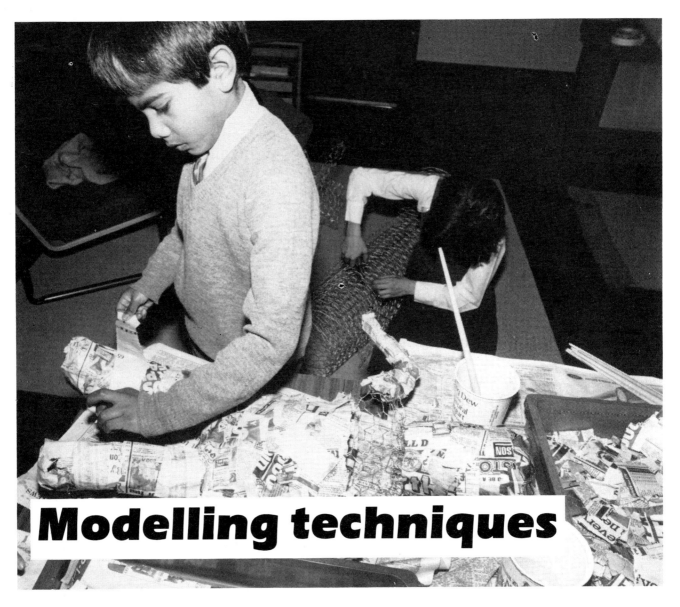

Modelling techniques

Basic animal shape

This basic animal shape, can be adapted to any four-legged creature. It will also develop the children's ability to stick awkward shapes together.

Two cuboids and four short cylinders of the same length form the basic shape. The cylinders could be two cardboard roll inners cut in half. First cover all the shapes with white kitchen paper, using paste. Encourage the children to stick all the edges well down. Stick the smaller cuboid above one end of the larger one, this time using white glue. Allow it to dry completely. Meanwhile paint the cylinders which will be the legs. When they are dry, make 2.5 cm snips at 2.5 cm intervals round one edge of each cylinder:

Stick the legs on using white glue and then, when dry, the children can select a suitably coloured and textured wool to wind around the body and head for hair or fur. Scraps of felt, sequins, pipe-cleaners etc should be available for adding extra features.

This idea could be adapted to make people – robots would look effective covered in silver foil or painted in metallic paint. Cones and cylinders are useful shapes for young children to make figures. Balls of white paper can be inserted in one end of a cylinder or cone for the head, art straws can be poked through or wound around the shape for arms, and children can choose from a selection of fabrics and wool for hair and clothes. Large-sized figures can be made in this way if the cone is first made from a semicircle of card.

This is an ideal opportunity for children to discuss their choices – which should not result in their choosing what the adult had in mind in the first place, however tempting that might be!

Egg-boxes can be adapted particularly well to animal shapes. The boxes can form bodies, with the bumps suggesting particular features: eg the scales of a dragon or dinosaur. Details such as necks, heads and tails can be cut from sugar-paper and attached by cutting slits in the egg-boxes. These may be painted using slightly thickened powder paint. Try making winding snakes from single strips of egg-boxes, fastened at intervals with papier mâché.

Using papier mâché

Egg-boxes can also be used to make moulding material. It produces a lumpy kind of papier mâché but it is easier to make and work than conventional papier mâché.

Tear fibre egg-boxes into very small pieces, put them in a bowl of hot water, and leave them to soak for 48 hours, stirring occasionally. Drain off the water but do not squeeze the mixture. Sprinkle on a teaspoon of cold water paste (without fungicide) and work the mixture until it is evenly distributed. Allow the mixture to stand for 15 minutes, then add one teaspoon of Polyfilla and knead the mixture again. It can now be used to form whatever shape is required. Let the shape dry thoroughly and then paint it, adding appropriate detail. Finish with a coat of varnish.

Older children may then be ready to experiment a little further. For example, seven- and eight-year-olds could cope well with making balloon masks using the following, papier mâché technique.

Blow up a round balloon and cover it with grease. Tear up pieces of newspaper about 2 to 3 cm long. Dip them in water and completely cover the balloon. Subsequent layers will require paste to stick them down. Cover the balloon with three or four layers of newspaper and finish with a layer of white kitchen paper. It is very important that the pieces of paper should not be too big and that all edges are well stuck down.

Leave the balloon to dry thoroughly, then burst it and cut the remaining shape in whatever way you like. It could make two masks, cut straight down the middle, or one to fit over the head. Paint it and add features.

Newspaper is used to build up a papier mâché figure.

Perhaps the children might adapt this basic idea to making animals with round and long balloons. The final shape could be left in one piece and sections of cardboard tubes added for legs.

Papier mâché built up around bottles can be made into figures. For this, paper strips are dipped in water and wound around a greased bottle until it is completely covered except for the base. Further strips are dipped in paste and added in the same way until four layers have been completed. When dry the bottle can be removed. A head can be made by twisting a ball of paper into the neck space and building up the join with layers of paper and paste. When all the papier mâché is dry, the figure can be painted and varnished.

For a more sophisticated version, form the figure on a wire structure. Before embarking on this children would benefit from observing the human body in different kinds of action such as jumping, running, kicking, dancing etc.

Make the framework by bending thin wire and embedding it in a block of wood. Put criss-cross strips of paper dipped in paste over the structure until the whole figure is built up. Paint and varnish it when it is dry. Strips of gauze dipped in plaster of Paris could be substituted for the paper, in which case it need not be painted.

The basic structure can be moulded from chicken wire.

Papier mâché can also be used to make puppets. Twist a ball of newspaper into the top of a cardboard tube. Dip small pieces of paper in paste and cover the initial shape with several layers. Make features exaggerated by pushing fingers into the shape and building it up where required. Finish with a layer of white paper. As before the pieces should be small and stuck well down. Paste strips around the neck, to join and make it secure. Paint the head when it is dry and add hair etc. Cut the cardboard tube down to about 4 to 5 cm in height and gently pull out the original newspaper leaving a hollow for the hand to work the head. Make the glove section from felt or other fabric by either sticking or sewing the edges together. Stick this to the top of the cardboard tube to make a neck.

Using tissue-paper

Another kind of model – rather like a kite – can be made from tissue-paper. Put two sheets of tissue-paper together, one on top of the other. Draw a fish, using as much of the paper as possible. Cut out the two pieces of tissue-paper together, making the mouth in the form of a semicircle. Stick on small pieces of paper to represent scales and eyes.

Stick the two sides together all round the edge of the fish's body. Make a circle out of wire and adjust it to the size of the circle formed by the fish's mouth.

Add streamers to the fish's body and a thin string to the wire. The body will fill with air and float.

You can also use tissue-paper to make an accurate model of a human face. Place a piece of white tissue-paper over the face, holding it in place with a piece of brown sticky parcel tape. Put a length of the tape all around the child's face and under the chin. Make two air holes at the nostrils so that the child can breathe, and cover the face with small pieces of the tape, working from the outside inwards. Make sure all the edges are stuck down. Leave the nose until last. Remove the mask and allow it to dry off before trimming any surplus tissue-paper. Strengthen the edges with overlapping tape. It can be painted or, alternatively, it could be built up with a thick layer of Copydex and tissue-paper to give a rubbery texture and to make it stronger.

Using cardboard boxes

Working in pairs on a project can be a valuable experience in terms of co-operation and discussion. A good subject for this would be a 'scene' in a large cardboard box of a model shop or house.

For a boat scene, line a box inside and out with pasted paper to strengthen it. When this is dry, the sky and background can be painted on. Wave strips can be made from lengths of paper a little longer than the box and painted with watercolours. These should be slotted in the sides of the box to give an illusion of depth and movement. Make rocks, harbour, banks, beach etc from crumpled newspaper and paste.

The boats can be made from smaller cardboard packets (cereal or detergent boxes would be about the right size). Shape the hulls with lengths of thin card cut to the right size and shape for the sides of the boat. Masts can be old paintbrush handles or pot plant supports, and sails, if required, made from scraps of suitable fabric. Small people can be constructed from pipe-cleaners, and matchsticks and cotton will make the rigging. Add paper seagulls by suspending them with cotton from the top of the box. If the mast is higher than the box, cut the top away to accommodate the height.

Shops and houses can be similarly constructed. As before, the box should first be strengthened with pasted paper and windows cut out and covered with transparent plastic film to represent glass. Inside, decorate the walls with appropriate wallpaper or paint while details can be painted or stuck on. The outside of the box could be covered with rubbings from small bricks or a brick pattern painted and crayoned. A sheet of thin card folded in two can be stuck to the top of the box for a pitched roof and a small carton would make a good chimney.

Children enjoy making cardboard buildings.

If the model is to be a shop, make fittings from small boxes covered in white paper and painted. Goods for sale might be made from papier mâché, tissue-paper etc, and pipe-cleaner people can be dressed in scraps of fabric. Let the children develop as much detail as they like, perhaps working on the model for several days.

House furniture can be easily made from matchboxes and paper-fasteners. One matchbox, upended, covered in brown paper with a paper-fastener for a handle, makes a chest of drawers. Tiny white beads can be added for feet. Carpets could be felt and sticky-back plastic makes realistic plastic flooring. Children will enjoy using their imagination to think of other items and should be encouraged to develop their own ideas in this way.

If they are making a bus or tram, the children could draw windows with the faces of passengers stuck in appropriate places and advertisements could be stuck on the side, with the number and route on the front. If the vehicle is of a different time, the children could research the kinds of advertisements that were around then and the clothes people wore. Passengers for the top of a tram could be made from cones, as described earlier. Hats can be made from the bottom 2 cm cut from a yoghurt pot and stuck, bottom of the pot uppermost, on a circle of card. Plastic can be painted successfully either with a special paint, or with ordinary powder or ready mix if the plastic is lightly rubbed first with sandpaper.

Really large scale models could be made by a class group, perhaps with the help of parents or students. These models could become playground features, at least for a while. Large human figures or enormous animals (such as dragons, dinosaurs, or large 'wild' animals) are good subjects for the chicken wire and papier mâché method.

First the frame has to be cut from chicken wire and 'stitched' together with galvanised wire. Children cannot really manage this on their own but they can be involved in the preliminary drawings and plans. Each large section of the model can be made separately (eg neck, head, body, legs), and then brought together. It must be a

A large scale model could be created by a whole class, each group making a different section.

strong structure and able to stand steadily – the legs and feet need to be particularly sturdy. Build up the shape with sheets of newspaper and paste. Everyone can help with this – lots of layers will be needed. Let it dry out thoroughly and then paint it. (If it is to stand outside use enamel paints.) Do the background first, adding other details when it is dry.

Using balsa wood

Older children are fascinated with the idea of working models – these can range from the comparatively simple to those which involve quite sophisticated scientific principles.

Boats can be made to work quite simply with a paddle. First make the basic boat shape in balsa wood.

For the paddle, cut a small flat piece of balsa wood and place it inside an elastic band. Secure it with a piece of sticky tape. Twist the elastic band and attach it to pins on the boat (see illustration). Put the boat in water and release the twist. Which way does the elastic band have to be twisted to make the boat go forward?

Balsa wood is an ideal material for making more precise models which require quite careful planning and measurement. Use strips of it with thin dowelling to make a simple moving vehicle. First make a rectangle with the strips and develop it into a cuboid.

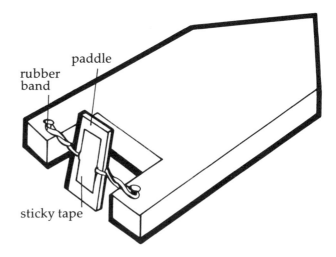

Use balsa cement to fix the strips and reinforce the joints with angles made from card. Make a smaller cuboid for the cabin of the vehicle in the same way and stick it

102

firmly to the first. Stick a triangle on each side at the bottom of the first cuboid and make holes to accommodate the dowelling which will function as the axle. Repeat this at the back. Cut circles of thin plywood for wheels and attach them to the dowelling.

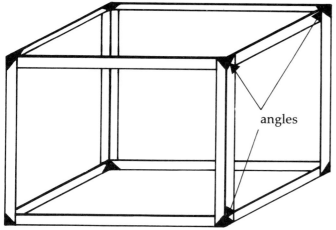

angles

Use card to complete the sides and bonnet of the vehicle and then it can be painted and varnished.

The basic idea of making cuboids from strips of balsa wood can be adapted to all kinds of models – buildings are particularly effective.

A different sort of working model can involve the principle of a simple electrical circuit. All that is needed for this is a couple of torch bulbs and bulb holders, a battery (4.5V) and a length of single strand bell wire.

You could make a model with eyes that light up or a vehicle with headlights or perhaps a lighthouse. First make the model with boxes in the same way as described earlier. Use strong cylinders if it needs legs (plastic bottles are useful). Egg-boxes, with the bottom cut away, make good light sockets. They can be covered with red tissue-paper for extra effect. Connect the two torch bulbs to a 4.5V battery using the bell wire. Children might need some help here as it is sometimes difficult for them to

manipulate a screwdriver. Place the holders in the sockets and test the lights. They can be disconnected by uncoupling one of the wires.

A dolls' house could be wired up in a similar way or you can make a lighthouse by fixing the circuit through a salt carton and a small jar: make the light flash by leaving a loose wire and repeatedly tapping it against the terminal of the battery. The jar is placed upside down on top of the bulb.

Younger children would probably enjoy making simpler models such as this crane made from a box, two knitting needles, thick card, two paper-fasteners, a cotton reel, a bent paper-clip and some thin string.

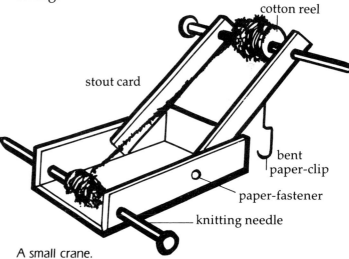

cotton reel

stout card

bent paper-clip

paper-fastener

knitting needle

A small crane.

There is a great deal of excitement in making models, whether they are to express emotional creativity, record information or apply some particular principle. It is important that the end result does not become too important – the learning process is the priority. Children are stimulated by work produced by other children and often inspired to develop an idea a little further, so the value of sharing learning cannot be stressed too strongly.

The ideas in this chapter are just a few to work on. Develop them yourselves and, most importantly, involve the children in the development.

Patterns

Patterns

INTRODUCTION

In daily life children are surrounded by patterns. In the man-made environment and in the natural world, patterns give pleasure and serve purposes.

From prehistoric times, man has felt the need to decorate his artefacts using ornamental patterns to enhance the appearance of utilitarian textiles, ceramics, household articles and buildings, or to endow important objects with some religious or ceremonial significance. Cultural traditions and fashions have defined the styles, and available materials

and tools have influenced the types of pattern produced.

However, it is not merely as decoration that patterns occur. Often they arise for practical reasons, related to the efficient use of space, time or energy; wall bricks and milk crates are arranged in an orderly fashion, and the bee builds a honeycomb of hexagons. As a means of communication, too, patterns may give warnings and signals, or attract the eye in order to impart information.

Learning about patterns spans the

urriculum, being firmly rooted in
mathematics, environmental studies and
some economics, and extends into the
realms of music, physical education and
language work.

However, teaching the subject of
pattern often tends to be rather piecemeal. A
more thorough and logical approach could
help to give the children an inspiration for
art and craft work, and will sharpen the
children's powers of observation. As with

other aspects of visual education, these
processes build up a sensitivity to beauty
and increase the faculties of constructive
criticism and artistic judgement. As an
extension to the more familiar
representational and expressive forms of art
and craft, the study of this aspect of design
contributes to every child's personal
development by introducing new concepts,
skills and qualities.

Starting points

Most of the concepts involved in making
patterns are easy for primary school
children to understand if they are explained
from the outset.

As with the teaching of reading or
mathematics, it is important to build on
what the child already knows, extending it
by logical steps and allowing ample time for
experimentation and practice at each stage.
Do not expect perfect results first time, and
do not be tempted to rush on to the next
idea too soon.

Work on patterns can begin in the
nursery where it will be an integral part of
play with sand, bricks, and constructional
toys, as well as in art and craft activities.
Early maths games and activities begin to
introduce basic concepts of pattern, and
everyday nursery experiences (threading
beads, sorting colours, arranging and
tidying equipment, setting the table)
present opportunities for early learning in
the subject.

Left to their own devices, children

under eight will make patterns in many different ways. They will call them 'patterns' because they are not representational pictures. Children of this age find it difficult to define a pattern, although they generally realise that shapes and colours are somehow involved, they may not yet have grasped the necessity for regularity in their arrangement. Given free rein they may produce circular and linear formations, coloured at random. Rarely before the age of seven will an 'untaught' child crayon a pattern which is symmetrical in both colour and shape. At this stage, the time is ripe for capturing their interest and introducing new ideas to enrich their work.

Older children become fascinated by detail and enjoy the satisfaction of producing an ordered design. Their growing experience of the use of colours and shapes enables them to organise abstract designs in imaginative ways. At the same time, their quest for realism in painting and drawing representational pictures can sometimes lead to a general lack of confidence in creative work. If their expertise does not match their expectations, their work may become stilted.

Taking refuge in producing precise, formal pattern may ease the child's immediate dilemma but it can be a time-wasting activity and could compound the problem. At this stage, particularly, the emphasis should be on creative pattern-making and the thoughtful production of unusual, individual designs.

Basic pattern-making

A pattern is a systematic arrangement of repeated components. They are constructed of lines and shapes, arranged in an orderly manner. Some say that a pattern must be constructed of identical parts arranged with rigid regularity, others detect elements of pattern in a collection of scattered, vaguely related shapes. The teacher must have a

good idea of the meaning of the word 'pattern' if children are to be taught about it.

The following basic ideas are the raw materials for pattern-making and provide the starting points for an introduction to the subject.

The repeated parts of a pattern must be recognisably similar to each other, and they

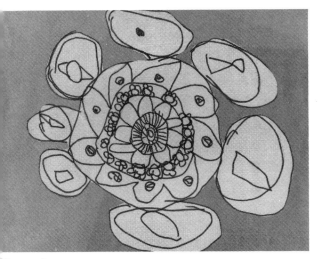

Figure 1

Figure 2

must be organised in a predictable way. A pattern is a design but not all designs are patterns (figures 1 and 2).

In the early stages of learning, the children need encouragement to observe and analyse patterns that they see around them. A walk round the school and local street looking for patterns is a sensible way to introduce the subject. Children will need help at first in discriminating between patterns and designs.

Basic pattern-making activities

• Sketch examples for discussion and for use in pattern-making later.
• Look for regular repetition in stitches and prints on clothes.
• Thread beads in regular patterns.
• For two children together: one starts a regular pattern, the other continues it.

Rigid repetition combined with absolute regularity can become boring if the design is not sufficiently eye-catching. Fortunately, the spontaneity and natural freedom of children's work often gives life to a design. Try to preserve this element without allowing slapdash work.

Lines

The simplest of all patterns is a line. By itself, a straight line is unexciting, but several together combine to make stripes, checks, tartans, networks and a multitude of individual shapes, each providing the potential for further embellishment with colours.

Decorated lines are vital to ornamental work and have been used to adorn pottery, textiles, stonework and wood for centuries.

Line patterns fall into five main groups:
• Zigzags: these can be evenly spaced but stretched out or closely packed, or they can be of varying size along the line.
• Waves and arches: try undulating and scalloped lines, in joined 'm', 'u' and 'c' shapes.
• Loops: these are usually lines which cross and loop in figures of eight.
• Keys and castles: these include lines which change direction with right angles, using repeated lines like the ends of keys or the battlements of castles.
• Spirals and scrolls: these are usually single or double-ended.

Lines can be produced with many materials – string, wrought iron, piped icing and any other continuous medium. They can be incised into wood, stone, clay and sand as they are often found in the natural world.

Because many of the movements involved in patterned lines are similar to those required for the formation of letter and number shapes, these 'writing patterns' should be practised by young children in conjunction with written work.

They can be further developed with different media and tools (pen and ink, chalk, fibre-tipped pens, thick and thin brushes and paint), thus serving the dual teaching purpose of aiding hand–eye co-ordination and improving handwriting skills, while introducing the basic elements of pattern work.

Line activities

- On a square piece of paper, draw straight and patterned lines, following the square shape (figure 3).

Figure 3

- Cut notches down the side of a crayon and draw with it edgeways.
- Paint scalloped, wavy and zigzag lines separately and intersperse each one with different colours.
- With a fibre-tipped pen, divide a sheet of paper into sections and draw a pattern with all kinds of lines (figure 4).

Figure 4

- Paint lines using big and small brushes, rollers and sponges.
- Make a string collage of spirals.
- Cut a spiral from circular paper, working from the outside inwards.

Shapes

Patterns are formed largely by arrangements of shapes or motifs. Sometimes these shapes

110

appear because of the crossing of lines (as in checks and diamond networks).

Certain motifs have been universally employed in ornamentation throughout the ages, in every part of the world. Among the most popular are: geometric shapes (triangle, circle, diamond, hexagon, rectangle); flowers (rose, lotus, chrysanthemum, tulip, daisy, fleur-de-lys); leaves (oak, laurel, ivy, acanthus, bay); fruit (pomegranate, pineapple, grapes on vine), and birds, animals, shells and hearts.

The shapes are drawn in a variety of forms, often simplified or stylised. Just as important as the chosen shapes are the spaces between them, which often become a vital part of the design.

Patterns made with shapes are to be found in every material – cloth, wood, clay, metal, plastic, concrete, stone and printed on paper. Looking at examples will help children to pick out the elements which form patterns, so that they can use them later in their own pattern-making.

Shape activities

- Make a classroom collection of designs from household objects and discuss the shapes which make up their patterns.
- Make a scrapbook of pictures of decorated objects, collecting patterns with similar shapes on each page: eg flowers, birds etc.

Figure 5

- Cut triangles out of fabric of one colour and make a collage pattern (figure 5).

Colour

Effective patterns can be made with a single colour on white, or with black on a coloured background. In these cases, contrast becomes an important feature. Two colours allow the use of counterchange (a pattern formed by repeating identical motifs alternately in two different colours) as on a chequer-board. A wide variety of two-colour designs is found in woven fabric, and in floor tiling and brickwork.

Patterns do not need colour, but many are enhanced by it. Where more colours are used, care must be taken to ensure that the structure of the pattern does not get lost in a welter of different hues and tones. Nevertheless, colour adds a different dimension, the same pattern coloured in different ways can look completely different.

Colour activities

Collect examples of two-colour patterns.
● Draw a counterchange pattern by dividing a symmetrical shape with vertical

and horizontal lines, then colour the corresponding parts in opposite colours (figure 6).

Figure 6

● Using paper of two colours, cut out squares; cut identical shapes from the squares and arrange them to make a counterchange pattern.
● Paint a simple pattern in shades of blue.

Arrangements

Lines and shapes can be organised in countless ways, but there are a few basic principles which will help the beginner. These are usually introduced in early mathematics activities, and can be consolidated and developed through art and craft.

A single shape can be manoeuvered by rotation, such as turning it round, moving it to different positions (as if round a clock face), placing it sideways, at angles, and upside down. It can also be moved by reflection, turning it over to make a symmetrical mirror image.

A number of shapes make patterns when they are touching or joining, overlapping, coloured in a sequence, alternating, in lines, in groups, or symmetrically arranged within a shape.

Arrangement activities

Combinations and permutations of these ways of organising shapes, and combining them with patterned lines offer children possibilities for unlimited, unique designs.
• Print a simple shape in lines, turning it round before each print; experiment with different shapes, one at a time (figure 7).

Figure 7

Figure 8

• Alternate two shapes to make a line of pattern.
• Experiment with rotating different shapes arranged in a line.
• Using sticky paper squares, investigate the many possibilities for arranging them in line – overlapping, touching and rotating (figure 8).

Looking for inspiration

Once the children get into the habit of looking for patterns around them, there is no shortage of inspiration for their own creative work.

Observing and analysing is the first step. Patterns can be recorded by sketches and rubbings, and photographs can be taken. The children are then ready to create their own patterns.

Encourage the children to ask themselves why the patterns they see around them are there at all. There are many answers: for safety, for efficiency, for information, or simply for pleasure.

Natural patterns

Patterns which occur naturally have several different causes and advantages. They act as warnings to predators and as signals to prospective mates. Flowers attract insects with pattern and colour; animals are camouflaged by stripes, spots and patches.

Polygons are often to be found in nature, as are branching patterns, spirals and radiating patterns. Underlying the infinite variety of patterns in nature are a few mathematical principles: these are the natural laws of symmetry, proportion and geometry which make natural things beautiful to us.

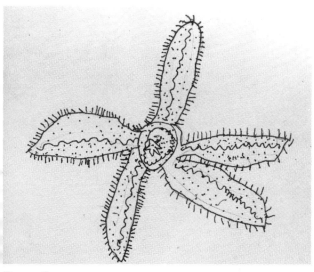

Figure 9

The microscope and the magnifying glass reveal patterns not normally noticed, so encourage their use. If living things are not available for observation, provide good pictures.

Patterns of every type will be found in natural things, such as animals (the zebra, tiger, leopard, tortoise), and sea creatures (shells, corals, sea urchins, starfish) (figure 9).

Insects and birds can be a good source of inspiration; try beetles (figure 10), butterflies, snails, and peacocks.

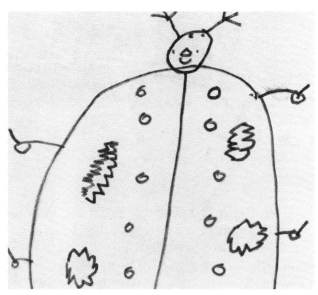

Figure 10

Take a close look at fish scales, plants (trees, bark, tree rings), leaves, pine cones, pineapples (figure 11), and segments of fruit and vegetables such as oranges (figure 12), kiwi fruit, cabbages and tomatoes.

Figure 11

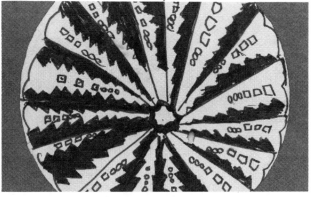

Figure 12

Figure 13

Study flowers, especially arrangements of petals; examine daisies, buttercups, pansies and poppies (figure 13); look at the hyacinth and foxglove on their stems. Cacti can provide a weird and wonderful array of patterns.

Other aspects of nature to examine include water, sand, rocks, stones and snow crystals.

Patterns in the home and at school

Perhaps the most obvious source of ideas for patterns is at home, where they are taken for granted. Examples of patterns influenced by past eras as well as modern designs are found in every household. A display of portable items borrowed from the children's homes will stimulate discussion and provide ideas, and the collection can be supplemented with pictures from magazines and catalogues.

Souvenirs from abroad give a glimpse of the pattern styles used in different countries.

Out of doors

Man-made patterns in the environment are usually purposeful. But fortunately, there is always room for creative pattern-making, even in mundane matters like building walls, and the wide variety of possible materials allows individuality in design.

Styles in architecture change with every decade and are reflected in ordinary housing as well as public buildings. The

Victorian era was rich in decorative detail – carved stonework, elaborate wrought iron, and fine brickwork – and the evidence remains in the streets of every town. In contrast, buildings of the twentieth century are less decorated; however, modern houses still present plenty of opportunities for work on patterns. Regional trends, too, may be apparent in the use of materials, particularly in brickwork designs and roofing.

Patterns used as signs make an interesting study for the older child. Logos and uniforms include symmetrical designs and blocks of patterns. Road markings are striking examples of pattern used to convey a message.

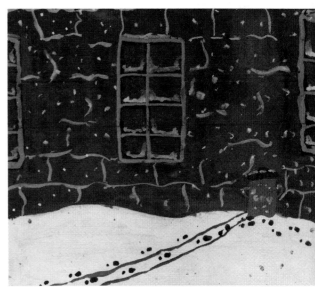
Figure 14

SLATES the way they are put on top of each other. And every one is the same shape

Figure 15

Many man-made patterns perform a particular function; help the children to bear this in mind when looking for patterns in their environment (figure 14). Try looking at particular aspects of buildings, such as walls and windows (panes, stained glass, and frames), doors, roof tiles (figure 15) and chimneys.

Examine scaffolding and piles of building material.

Look at the street, especially road markings and signs, and surrounding features like fences, railings and gates.

Manhole covers, paving and steps can provide inspiration as well as wheels, tyres and parked cars.

Shops contain stacked tins, piled fruit, trolleys, boxes and window displays; these can also be a good source of coloured patterns.

Developing pattern-making

When children understand the basic concepts of pattern-making and have had some experience of analysing patterns in their environment, they are ready to develop the more complex skills of pattern construction. At this stage, make sure that they understand words like 'repeat', 'regular', and 'alternate' (verb and adjective). Allow plenty of time for experimentation with techniques and colour combinations.

Bands and borders

Band patterns develop naturally from patterned lines. Extra strokes are added to a simple line to give a feathery or branched

appearance. A wavy line or a zigzag is embellished with shapes; 'key' and 'castle' lines are elaborated and broadened to make complicated fret patterns.

Variations of chain designs and plaits also make good bands. All patterned lines can be overlapped or placed closely together so that they interlock. Shapes formed where the lines cross can be coloured in, accentuating parts of the pattern which might not otherwise be noticed.

Lines of motifs are also used to form band patterns and borders – a band of daisy-heads, interspersed with leaves, for instance, or heart shapes placed alternately the right way up and upside-down. Joined and overlapped shapes create spaces in between, which become an integral part of the pattern.

Corners need special attention. In continuous small-scale patterns they present no problem, but if the band is formed from large motifs they have to be spaced evenly between the corners. A similar motif spreading round each corner gives the design continuity.

Border bands are useful for decorating children's written work, book covers and greetings cards, and to make frames for displays.

Band and border activities

When building up bands from patterned lines, encourage the children to work rhythmically, without stopping and starting more than necessary, and checking back to see that the size is fairly even. However, exact uniformity makes a pattern lifeless, so discourage the use of rulers and rubbers.
- Experiment with circles, arranging them in various ways to make bands (figure 16).

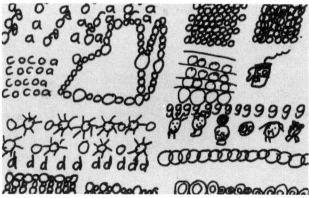
Figure 16

- Combine patterned lines, such as zigzags, to make a band by overlapping them; colour the spaces in between.
- Cut two sets of shapes out of paper or fabric and arrange them on a piece of card to form a frame for a picture (figure 17).

Figure 17

- Cut leaf shapes from fabric and place them alternately each side of a wavy line of fancy string or braid (figure 18).
- On openwork fabric, use simple embroidery stitches to make a table mat.
- After looking at examples, design a border for a lace curtain.

All-over patterns

Small, all-over patterns, such as floral prints of tiny flower sprigs, often seem to be

Figure 18

116

scattered or 'powdered' at random, but there will always be a repeated section unless the design is hand-painted.

Similarly, designs formed from trailing and interwoven foliage may not appear at first sight to be constructed to a plan, but closer inspection usually reveals that they are organised within a patterned framework.

Continuous patterns designed to cover a large surface include stripes (repeated bands, plain and patterned, wide and narrow), tartans, and checks. Networks can also be included: these involve geometric outlines, such as diamonds, hexagons, triangles, etc, tessellating to form an overall framework for motifs.

Figure 20

Figure 19

Regular patterned lines, placed close together, are the basis of many all-over designs and are a simple way of creating networks. Zigzags form diamonds if drawn with their points touching; wavy lines form ogees (pointed ovals) if drawn with their bulges touching (figure 19); arched lines form scale patterns if moved half a space sideways so that the points of one line meet the curves of the next (figure 20).

More complicated networks of tessellating or interlocking shapes can be built on a basic square net; rectangles, polygons and unusual shapes can be produced by combining and subdividing the squares. Similarly, a network of triangles or diamonds offers a wide variety of larger shapes, forming hexagons, stars

and larger triangles. These networks of shapes are then embellished with further decoration and linked to form an all-over pattern.

All-over patterns run the risk of being dull if there is not sufficient detail and variety of colour, shape and line to interest the eye. A draught-board, for example, is a perfect but unimaginative pattern which does not please for long. However, if a check pattern is held at different angles, it takes on new interest: for example checked fabric is instantly more interesting if hung to fall in soft folds. If shades of grey as well as black and white are introduced or motifs placed in some of the squares, it immediately becomes livelier.

Slight variations in the colouring and placing of motifs in an all-over pattern add charm and life to a design. In 3D patterns, the effect of light and shade brings extra interest; the angle of the light can radically change the overall appearance of the design.

In all-over patterns based on repeated lines, the 'drop' is often employed. Instead of repeating the second line of pattern directly alongside the first, if is shifted half a space along, so that the motifs occur between rather than next to the previous ones. Normal brickwork shows the principle in a horizontal mode; many curtain materials and wallpapers are printed with vertical half-drop designs.

All-over pattern activities

Squared paper is useful for trying out regular designs before expressing them more freely; the spacing and placing of motifs can be sketched on a small scale before the final painting, collage or print is started.

Repeated motifs are most easily produced by printing, or by using shapes cut from paper folded to make several motifs at once. Sizes need not always match exactly and lines need not be straight, as long as the pattern is not seriously disrupted.

A useful 'spare moments' exercise involves colouring in the squares and parts of squares to form blocks of two-colour patterns (figure 21). This should inspire larger-scale work in other media. Plain paper or fabric may, of course, be marked out with guidelines in pencil, or folded to give the necessary framework for a design.

A co-operative pattern can be carried out by children working simultaneously on one large background, or by assembling smaller pieces of individual work to make one large pattern.

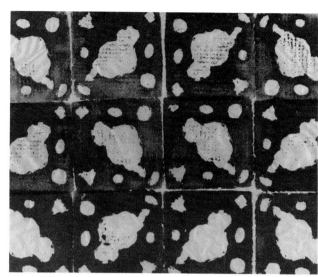
Figure 22

another design (figure 24).
• Using diagonal stripes as guidelines, stick shapes cut from coloured paper squares in stripes (figure 25).
• Draw or paint a pattern based on wavy lines with motifs in the spaces formed.
• Printed fabrics can be made into bags, aprons, pin cushions and clothes for puppets.

Enclosed patterns

Many patterns are designed to fit a specific area – a window, a box top, a circular tin tray – and are contained within the shape.

Figure 21

• For young children, finger painting provides opportunities for quick and free pattern-making; a print can be taken and the design adapted to make more patterns.
• Use an irregular motif to print a tile pattern, rotating it each time (figure 22).
• With a design on a printing block, print a pattern by placing each square directly next to the last. Then, using the same block, move each half-way along the last side printed to make a 'drop' pattern (figure 23).
• Fold a large piece of paper into squares and paint a design in alternate spaces. Fill the other spaces with plain colour or

A pattern is enclosed within a triangular shape.

118

An all-over pattern is always possible in these cases, but more often than not the space is divided into two or more parts, and those parts decorated.

For these enclosed patterns, or patterns within shapes, the most common subdivisions are: circles (concentric rings or a central motif and border design); you could also try a wavy line across the diameter; radiating segments such as petal shapes and spirals. Squares, rectangles, and polygons can also be subdivided into smaller areas.

Figure 25

Enclosed pattern activities

- Give the children shaped paper for their circular, square and triangular patterns; they will learn how the outline shape dictates the type of design. Each section of the pattern should be ornamented with patterned lines and motifs. Later, let the children experiment with odd shapes (figure 26).

Figure 26

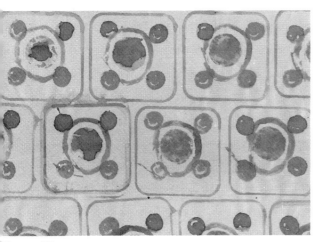

Figure 23

- Divide a circle into segments and decorate them (figure 27).
- Design a rug with a border.
- Cover a cardboard box and lid with paper; plan patterns to fit the side and lid, to make a gift box.

Figure 24

Figure 27

119

Symmetrical designs

A shape or pattern which can be divided down the centre so that both sides match exactly is symmetrical. Some (a square, for example) can be divided on more than one axis and still be symmetrical. A circle is symmetrical whichever way you look at it.

Symmetry is a vital concept in pattern-making, as is balance: designs are sometimes constructed so that they are not strictly symmetrical, but similar shapes of comparable size are placed so that the overall design looks well-balanced.

Symmetrical designs often occur in folk art. A favourite motif is the vase of stylised flowers and leaves, gaily coloured, as a decoration on wooden furniture or embroidered on linen. It is perhaps a version of the older symmetrical design known as the 'tree of life', which originated in ancient Assyria and is still used for Polish paper cuts. In this design the tree is given leaves, exotic fruits and birds, and on the hillock at its roots stand a pair of animals; it symbolises the universe.

Figure 29

Symmetrical design activities

- The easiest way for children to understand symmetry is by folding and cutting paper to make shapes of increasing complexity. These may be coloured to reinforce the symmetry of the design.
- 'Blot' painting, where paper is folded on to thick paint blobs, gives some idea of symmetrical design, as does string printing, where a pattern is formed by pulling paint-soaked string between folded paper. Creating a reflecting pattern from scratch (by drawing, printing or collage) is much more demanding, requiring concentration and judgement, particularly where curved lines and spirals are involved.
- Use a mirror to look at the reflection of drawn shapes.
- Write a word in bold letters and draw its reflection to make a symmetrical design (figure 28).
- Arrange small matching shapes symmetrically on a background paper with a central vertical fold; embellish the pattern with coloured lines and further decoration, to make a vase of flowers or a butterfly's wings (figure 29).
- Paint a 'tree of life'.

Figure 28

Using different techniques

All art and craft materials can be used in creating patterns. The choice of technique for making patterns influences the success of the result, and each material has its advantages, disadvantages and special effects. A wide range of colours is not always necessary in order to produce patterns; in most cases, the structure of the pattern is emphasised if it is carried out in only two or three colours.

Experiment by combining techniques: collage with painting; crayons and printing; paper cutting with stencilling; needlework and collage.

Sketching

Teach the children to sketch, using a soft pencil and light strokes, drawing rough outlines of shapes and mere indications of lines. The technique is useful for making visual notes of ideas and for planning patterns of all kinds. Encourage free-hand drawing of straight lines and circles. For further ideas, see the chapter on 'Drawing' on pages 1 to 16.

Wax resist

Draw heavily with wax crayons and wash over the pattern with ink, which will give a richness to the design (figure 30). Effective black and white designs are made using an ordinary white candle and black ink. See page 129 in the chapter on fabric for further details.

Rubbings

Making a rubbing is a useful way of recording patterns *in situ*. Cover the surface with a sheet of paper and fix it with masking tape. Using firm strokes, scribble heavily with wax crayons in order to make a dark impression. This is also detailed in the 'Printing' chapter on page 158.

Figure 30

Painting

Fold the paper into squares or mark out networks if necessary. Try restricting the range of colours, or use shades of one colour. For large areas, thicken the paint by adding paste.

White paint on black paper is effective for interpreting natural patterns. For further ideas, see the chapter on 'Painting' on pages 19 to 33.

Finger painting

Spread mixed cold-water paste directly on to the paper, and add dry powder paint with the fingers (use the primary colours and white). The paste may also be 'combed' with a serrated piece of card or plastic.

To take prints, place a sheet of thin paper on the finished pattern, smoothing it down lightly before peeling it off.

Printing

Make use of materials such as cardboard tubes, small boxes and lids, metal shapes, sponges, corks, cotton reels, leaves and potatoes. Make your own printing blocks from wood or polystyrene, with the design made out of string (figure 31), corrugated cardboard, or the foam back of a carpet with shapes picked out with a pin.

For large areas of pattern, mark out guidelines by chalking a string, holding it taught and pinning it against the fabric.

Good patterns can be made with one main colour on a coloured background. Complicated blocks are not essential to an effective pattern; many variations are possible by rotating a simple design. Build up a collection of printing blocks, for use in different combinations. Further ideas on 'Printing' can be found on pages 154 to 165.

Stencils

For reproducing identical shapes on a white background, cut the design out of the centre of a piece of card; older children could use craft knives rather than scissors. Paint through the hole, moving it along to a new position each time.

Alternatively, for a white design surrounded by colour, cut a piece of card into the required shape, and brush paint across the outside edge of the card. Patterned lines can be produced in this way, for a scalloped or zigzag edge to the card.

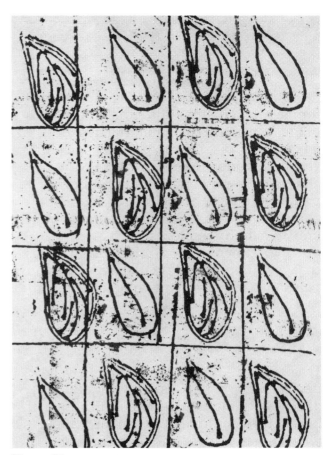

Figure 31

Collage

When making collage patterns, encourage the children to cut out several shapes at the same time. A cardboard template cut to the required shape by the child is a help. Small pieces, and lengths of string, are best stuck by applying the glue to the paper and dropping the material on to it. See the chapter on 'Collage' on pages 35 to 49.

Cut paper

Remind the children to keep the folds intact if making a single pattern. Paper patterns can be unfolded and refolded in a different direction for more exciting results. Several can be assembled together as a display.

Cut identical shapes out of a sheet folded into eight or sixteen and arrange them to form the basis of a pattern.

Torn paper can be equally interesting.

Clay

For incised and impressed patterns scratch lines into the clay and press small objects into it to leave dents. Pieces left in the clay will fall out when the clay dries, or burn in the kiln.

For applied patterns add coils and small balls of clay to the surface, joining them securely.

A class could make a set of patterned tiles, which are fired or left to dry before being varnished. See the chapter on 'Clay' for further ideas, on pages 73 to 93.

Tie and dye

The cloth (figure 32) is tied with string in folds or clumps so that parts remain undyed when it is immersed in the dye bath (see pages 129 and 132).

Different patterns are made in the following ways:
- concentric circles: pick up the centre point of the fabric and tie it at intervals;
- small circles: tie buttons into the fabric;
- stripes: fold concertina-style and tie at intervals. The tie and dye technique is detailed on page 129.

Needlework

Combine simple stitches to make circular and linear motifs. Sew on beads and sequins for added interest. Several small panels could be made by a group of children and combined to make a 'patchwork'. See the chapter on needlework on pages 51 to 70.

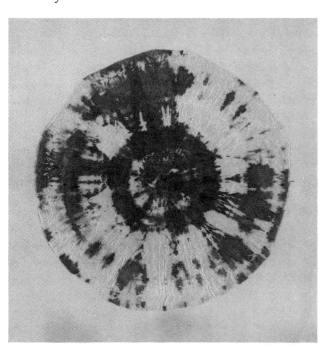

Figure 32

Children have impressed patterns into their clay work.

Weaving

Early experimentation with weaving leads young children to an understanding of the many possibilities for woven patterns. Start with two colours and 'under one, over one' to produce a check, and then explore the variations. A chapter on weaving can be found on pages 167 to 181.

Further development

There is enormous scope for developing every aspect of the subject of pattern.

Different techniques and materials can be experimented with for large and small-scale work using every sort of pattern. The basic types can be elaborated and new combinations generated mathematically and by computer.

Older children are capable of pursuing the many facets of pattern in their environment. Countless topics encountered by children in school – from the peasant's fishing net to the heat-shield tiles on a space ship – demonstrate the universal applications of pattern. It is an integral part of life, and as such is worthy of a place on the timetable in the education of every child.

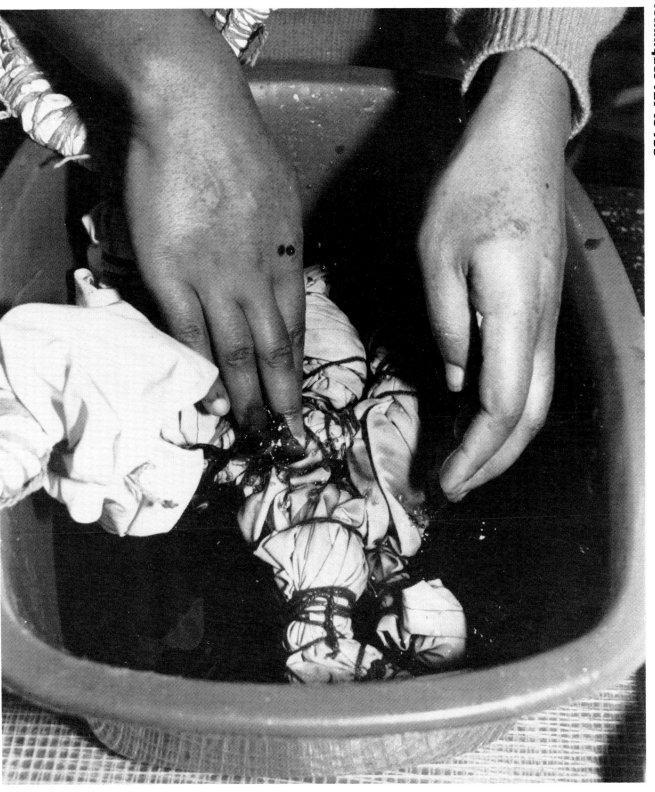

Fabric and dyeing techniques

Fabric and dyeing techniques

INTRODUCTION

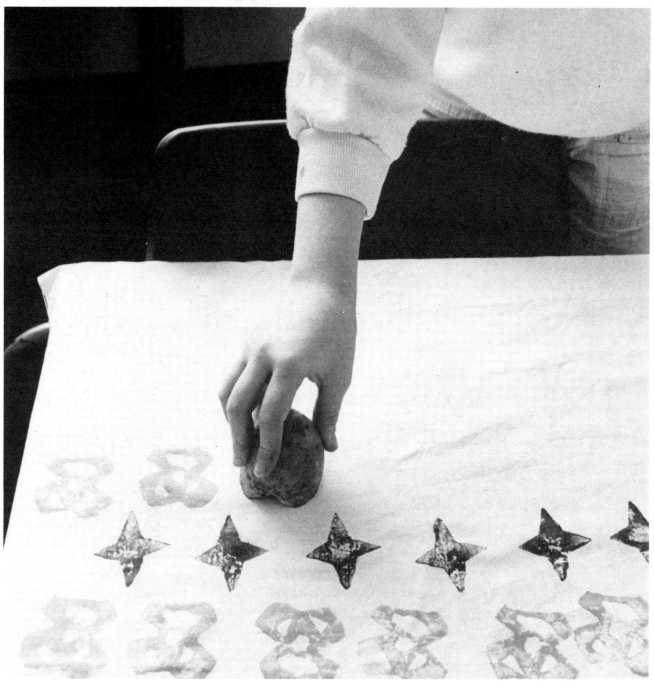

There are many different ways of working with fabrics and dyes to create exciting and colourful results. The standard techniques of tie dyeing, Batik and printing can be combined with more experimental methods for a livelier approach and more varied end products.

Projects can be undertaken on an individual or group basis, and no expensive equipment is needed.

Tie dyeing

Tie dyeing is one of the oldest and simplest methods of decorating fabric.

It is a resist technique created by tying, knotting or sewing areas of fabric together to keep the dye out. The Malaysian name for tie dyeing is *plangi*. Tie dyeing is the safest and cheapest method of working with fabric and is particularly suitable for children from the age of eight upwards to experiment with.

You will need the following materials: cold water dyes and fix, salt, bowls for dye, well-washed cotton fabric, string, cotton twine or raffia, scissors, overalls and rubber gloves, and a line to dry the fabrics on.

To give different effects the fabric can be used wet or dry. Mix the dye in a bowl. Always carefully read the instructions on the dye-cans before use. The simplest way is to knot the fabric at the corners or along the length. Place it in the dye bowl for a short time (if you leave it for too long the effect is

less dramatic), rinse it in cold water, squeeze it out and hang it up to dry. A drying cabinet is particularly useful to speed up the process. When the fabric is dry unknot and iron it to see the effect created.

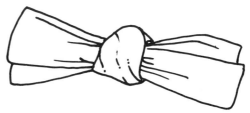

Tying with string

Many methods of folding and tying fabric can be used to create different effects.

A combination of two methods used on the same piece of fabric or a repeat tying

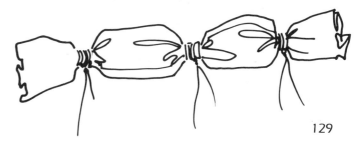

129

using a second dye will give more interesting results.

A marble pattern can be achieved by tying with string. This is most effective with damp fabric. Take a piece of fabric and, working from the centre, crumple it all together until it forms a ball. Tie the ball all round with string and knot the end leaving a long tail of string by which to hold the ball. Place it in the dye bath for a little longer than the knotting method, remove it, allow it to dry and untie it. Marbelling is most effective if the process is repeated several times with different colours.

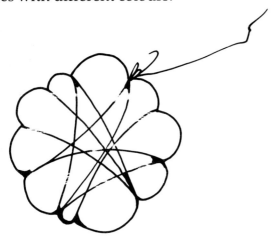

To make circles, pick up the centre of a piece of fabric and smooth the rest down like a closed umbrella. Bind string tightly along the length of the fabric varying the distance between the bound areas and the depth of each binding. Secure the end of the string and place it in the dye bath. Leave it in the bath for at least ten minutes. Remove the fabric wearing rubber gloves, rinse it, squeeze it and leave it to dry. When it is dry untie the binding and iron the fabric (unless you wish to re-dye in a second colour).

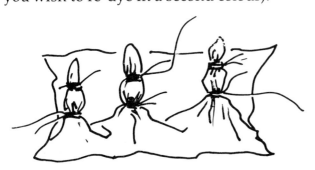

Small circles can be achieved by the same method as the large circles. Pick up the fabric and tie string around the diameter, repeating several times over the piece of fabric.

When re-tying a piece of fabric repeat the process completely making sure that both areas of white and the first colour are covered with binding for the best effect. Leave on some of the original bindings if you wish.

To make a chequered pattern, fold a piece of fabric in a concertina shape and tie string across the length at intervals. Leave the fabric in the dye for a shorter time when using this method.

For double folding, fold the fabric in a concertina shape and fold again into a small parcel. Tie string tightly around the parcel.

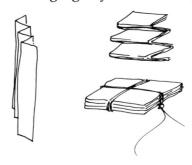

If you tie beads or buttons in the fabric you will get a pattern of tiny circles.

Clothes pegs can be used to create interesting patterns. Fabric can be folded completely or just around the edges and ordinary household pegs used to resist the dye.

Batik

Batik is not only fun to do, but also useful as a practical demonstration of colour mixing. For example, yellow fabric put in blue dye makes green, and yellow fabric put in red dye makes orange.

Batik is a traditional Javanese technique involving the use of wax or starch as a dye resist. The wax is painted, and thrown on to the fabric either with a brush or a special tool called a 'tjanting'. The fabric is then either dip dyed or painted with dye. The wax 'resist' repels the dye so that areas painted with wax remain the original colour. A particular feature of batik is the crackle effect which can be achieved by cracking the wax before putting it into the dye bath.

Batik is more suitable for older children, particularly as hot wax is used. You will need the following materials for successful results: a waterless wax heater, tjantings or/and brushes, cold water dyes and fix, bowls for dye, frames to stretch fabric or plastic sheets, white cotton, calico or cheesecloth, wax (ordinary household candles or blocks).

Stretch the fabric over a frame and use drawing-pins to secure it in place. Old picture frames can be used or special adjustable batik frames can be bought or made. Alternatively fabric can be taped on to plastic sheeting or waxed kitchen paper. Lightly pencil your chosen design on to the fabric.

Mix the dyes in bowls large enough to take several pieces of fabric at once. Cold dyes are suitable for batik and can be bought in special batik colours which are particularly vibrant. Test the strength of the dye and hang a strip of fabric over the side of the bowl to indicate the colour of each one.

Place the wax in the heater. Waterless heaters are specially designed not to overturn and are far safer than double boilers. The wax must be hot enough to soak right into the fabric, not just to sit on the surface.

Apply hot wax to the areas which you wish to remain the original fabric colour (usually white). Use a tjanting for fine lines and a brush for large areas. The wax should look transparent when applied to the fabric. If it appears milky white it is not yet hot enough.

The first dye colour should be the lightest one. With batik always work in stages from light through to dark. The fabric is traditionally fully submerged in the dye bath. However it may be more convenient to paint areas with dye using a large soft household brush. Before doing so the wax can be cracked by squeezing in the hand, this allows thin lines of dye into the waxed areas. The fabric must be hung up to drip dry. It cannot be artificially dried because any heat will melt the wax and ruin the design. Batik is best handled over several lessons, one colour per lesson. The rest of the time can be spent experimenting with tie dye techniques.

When it is completely dry re-stretch the fabric on the frame and wax over all areas which you wish to remain the colour of the first dye. Place the fabric in a second dye bath, remove it, and then leave it to dry.

Repeat the process one more time with a third dye.

To remove the wax, iron the fabric between sheets of kitchen paper or old newspapers. As soon as a sheet becomes soaked with wax replace it with a clean one until no more wax can be ironed off. The fabric can then be washed with hot water and detergent to remove the remaining wax.

Fabric is stretched over a frame and pinned in place.

Other batik methods

A safer, though not so reliable method of resist dyeing is to use flour and water instead of wax. Mix the flour and water to a paste and paint it on to the fabric in the same way as the wax. It is better to paint the dye on to the fabric as the paste begins to break down with repeated submersion in the dye bath.

An interesting way to experiment with resist dyeing is to paint wax on to paper. Cartridge paper, coloured inks or powder paint can be used instead of dye.

Fabric printing techniques

Monoprinting

Monoprinting is a simple method of transferring an image on to fabric and can be used in conjunction with spraying or printing with objects (see page 132).

You will need the following materials: sheets of heavy perspex or glass, rollers, fabric printing ink, brushes, white cotton or calico.

The ink is painted on to a sheet of glass to create any design or picture, so any number of colours can be painted on at the same time.

Place the fabric evenly over the glass right side down and use the roller to press firmly over the whole surface.

Peel the fabric off the glass and the transferred image will appear.

It is possible to repeat the process with another piece of fabric. You will get a fainter image with each successive print.

Stencils can also be cut and placed on the glass to achieve a different kind of image. For this technique an even coat of ink should be applied to the glass with a roller and pieces of cut paper scattered or gently placed on top of the ink.

Carefully lay the fabric over all of the glass and apply pressure with a clean roller.

The area covered by the stencil will remain white. This method can be repeated several times to build up an interesting design.

Instead of using specially cut stencils other materials can be put on to the prepared ink surface as long as they are not too thick. For example, string, cotton, wool, small pieces of textured fabric, matchsticks etc.

Spraying

Combined with stencil-making, spraying is one of the most immediate ways of making marks on fabric. So that minimum mess is created, keep cold water dyes mixed in plastic spray bottles.

You will need the following materials: plastic spray bottles (one for each colour), paper or card for stencils, scissors, and white cotton or calico.

First cut interesting shapes from paper and place them on the fabric. Then spray evenly over the fabric holding the container as upright as possible. Use several colours and move the stencils to create overlapping patterns and to cover the whole fabric with designs.

A softer effect can be created by dampening the fabric first, which will enable the colours to merge together. Masking tape can be placed on fabric to create a striped design. Articles such as pencils, pieces of string, bottle tops etc can also be used as stencils. Remember to wipe them afterwards.

As with other dyeing techniques, spraying is more effective if repeated using several colours.

Block printing using polystyrene

Block printing is one of the most versatile methods of transferring an image on to fabric. Any objects or materials which can be attached to the block can be used to create a variety of interesting images. A particularly interesting method is to use textured wallpapers.

Blocks of polystyrene (about 2.5 cm thick and 15 cm square) can be purchased or cut from packaging material. Use pins to attach the objects to the block (not suitable for younger children). You will also need fabric printing ink, ink rollers, white cotton or calico and a sheet of perspex to roll the ink on.

Place the polystyrene block on a working surface and arrange a design using objects with interesting textures. Pin through the objects to secure them to the polystyrene block. Roll the ink on to the sheet of perspex and continue rolling to ensure an even coat of ink on the roller.

Carefully holding the edges of the polystyrene block, roller ink over the arranged objects to ensure all the raised surfaces are coated. Place the fabric over the block and press it with a clean roller.

Alternatively, fabric can be laid on a clean table with a block placed face down on to it. Then roller the back of the block. If covering a large area of fabric the second method is more suitable.

Lift the inked block from the fabric to view the result. You will be able to tell whether too much or too little pressure was used on the roller. The polystyrene block can be used repeatedly, with different objects in various arrangements to create a pattern or a picture. Textured fabrics, hessian, carpet, lace, leaves, wood shavings, string, cotton, wool, plastic mesh bags, corrugated cardboard, cut-out card shapes as well as textured wallpapers are ideal materials for block printing.

Designs can be cut out of the block so that only the raised surface receives the ink. However the block cannot be used again for other designs.

Pressing with a clean roller.

Potato printing, a simple technique, is surprisingly effective, but take care with cutting.

Potato printing

Potato printing is a traditional way of introducing printing. Care has to be taken if allowing young children to cut their own potatoes. It is better if you cut several designs on to potatoes first and then give them to the children to experiment with on pieces of fabric.

You will need several good-sized firm washed potatoes, a sharp knife, fabric printing ink, rollers, an inking surface, white cotton or calico.

Cut a potato in half lengthways. Draw a design on to the exposed surface and mark a line about 6 mm down from the surface all the way round the diameter of the potato. Holding the potato firmly in one hand cut 6 mm down all the way round the design drawn on the potato surface. Try to keep to the lines. When the outline has been cut downwards, cut from the side along the diameter line and remove the flesh to leave the design raised from the new surface. The potato is then ready for printing.

Prepare at least one half potato for each child to use; if the designs are different they can swap about during the lesson to try combining images to create patterns.

The potato is then simply used as an ink pad, stamped on to a well-inked surface, then on to stretched out fabric.

Direct printing with objects such as jam jars, bottle tops, lids, sponges, pencils, pieces of carrot, matchboxes or other small

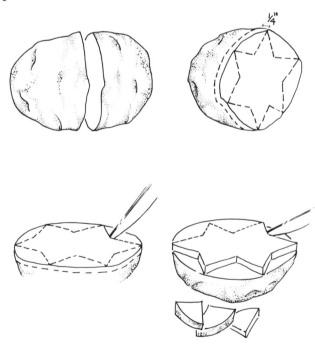

Preparing a potato for printing.

containers, and empty cotton reels can be very effective. In the same way as the potato they are pressed on to the ink pad, then on to the fabric for instant results.

Other methods of printing using more complex techniques are lino and wood-block printing.

Tissue-paper printing

A simple method of colouring fabric is by using coloured tissue-paper which releases its dye when wet.

All ages will enjoy this method of printing. You will need very few materials: coloured tissue-paper, scissors and white cotton or calico.

Cut out stars, circles, squares or any shape from the tissue-paper. Wet the fabric, wring it out and spread it out on a clean surface. Place the tissue-paper shapes on to the fabric to create a picture or pattern.

Starting from one end, roll the fabric up as tightly as possible keeping the tissue-paper in position. When it is completely rolled up, squeeze tightly along the length. This will ensure that the tissue-paper becomes well soaked and the dye will transfer to fabric.

Unroll the fabric and remove the tissue-paper. This can be repeated with more colours until the fabric is covered with patterns.

Painting fabric

Painting directly on to fabric is a quick and easy method without using costly materials or complicated equipment.

Special paint or dyes, or even ordinary dyes, can be used with special paste added to thicken them for easier handling. Small stiff brushes are best for detailed work (bristle brushes are ideal) and soft large brushes for bigger areas. You will also need water pots and containers for the dyes, cotton or calico (well-washed to remove stiffening), frames and drawing-pins or white paper, and a fanheater or hairdryer.

The fabric should be stretched on a frame and secured using drawing-pins. If this is not possible sheets of paper should be placed under fabric to prevent the dyes seeping through on to the tables.

Draw the design faintly on the fabric using a soft-leaded pencil. Fill in the large areas of colour first, and use a hairdryer or fanheater to dry these before filling in the finer details.

Using small, thin brushes, add the finer details. Experiment by allowing the colours to blend on the fabric. Allow the dyes to dry before removing the fabric from the frame or backing paper.

You can also work on wet fabric which will blend the colours together. For thinner or lighter colours dilute the dyes with water.

Press or mirror printing

An interesting experiment with hand-painting fabric inks is mirror printing.

Divide the fabric in half, paint patterns on to one half and while it is still wet fold the other half over on top of the pattern. Press the clean side of the fabric down on to the other using a clean roller. When it is opened up you have a mirror image on each side of the fabric.

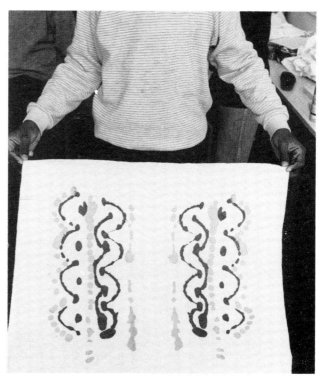

Mirror printing.

135

Yarn

Yarn

INTRODUCTION

How or when knitting began no one knows for certain. Examples of knitted fabric have been found in Egyptian tombs, Scandinavian peat bogs have revealed knitted scraps dating from 15 BC, and it is thought that knitting came to Britain with the invaders of the fifth and sixth centuries AD. In the Middle Ages there were knitting guilds; an apprentice, after studying the craft for six years, would have to produce a shirt, a felted cap, a pair of socks, and a knitted carpet before he could become a guild member.

However, what is certain today is that the crafts of knitting and crochet are enjoying a revival, and that with it there is a renewal of interest in the scope and possibilities that the craft affords.

The classroom can provide the children with the opportunity to see a process from raw materials to the finished product.

Achieving success will be the starting point for more ambitious work, and first attempts will need encouragement. When teaching how to knit and crochet, do cast on for the beginner to knit at least the first row,

s this will help considerably. You may also
ind it an advantage to start with two
lifferent coloured needles – it can help
vhen talking through a technique.

Do try and make any piece of knitting,
vhether it is a first attempt or an advanced
project, into something worth while. The
knitter will then see the result of their efforts
and will hopefully 'knit on', improving their
techniques, and building on their
understanding of the very old crafts of
knitting and crochet.

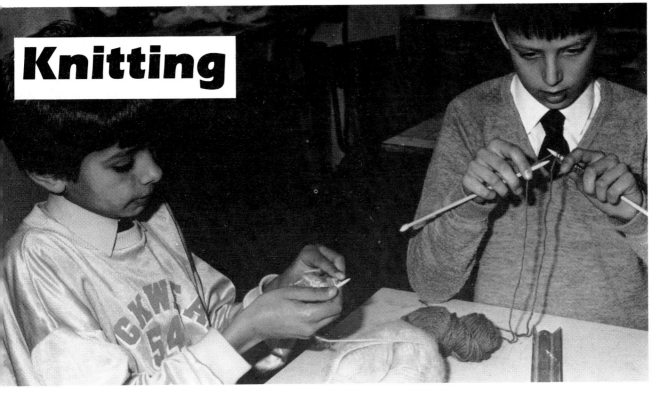

Knitting

Yarns

Yarns in every colour, composition and
texture can be found in the shops today, but
cut or torn strips of fabric, leather thonging,
raffia, tights, or even plastic waste disposal
bags may be used for knitting. However, it
is easier to learn by using a thick, smooth
yarn such as a double knitting or a chunky
knit on large needles. Avoid using fine or
knobbly yarns with the children until they
become more experienced.

Needles

Knitting needles are the main tools that are
needed. They used to be made from wood or
bone but are now made from lighter weight
materials such as coated metal or plastic.
Needles are available in a variety of sizes
and length, and are sold in pairs. The length
of needle you use depends on personal
choice and the size of the item you are

making. For small items, a 30 cm needle is
comfortable to use.

Needle sizes

Metric	British
2mm	14
2¼mm	13
2¾mm	12
3mm	11
3¼mm	10
3¾mm	9
4mm	8
4½mm	7
5mm	6
5½mm	5
6mm	4
6½mm	3
7mm	2
7½mm	1
8mm	0
9mm	00
10mm	000

Tension

Tension plays a vitally important part in knitting. If it is too tight, the fabric will be hard and the stitches will be too crowded, not showing to their best effect. If the work is to be washed, it will felt and shrink easily. If the tension is too loose, the fabric will be floppy and will not retain its shape.

It is always essential to make a tension test before commencing any piece of knitting to ensure that your personal tension suits the yarn and stitch pattern. It is important to remember that each person's knitting tension varies and that it is the individual tension of the designer that is quoted in a knitting pattern. If the pattern is knitted up in the wrong tension, it can result in work which is far too large or too small.

To check your tension, knit a 10 cm square. Count the number of stitches and rows to the centimetre. If there are too many stitches, use a size larger needle, if too few, a size smaller needle.

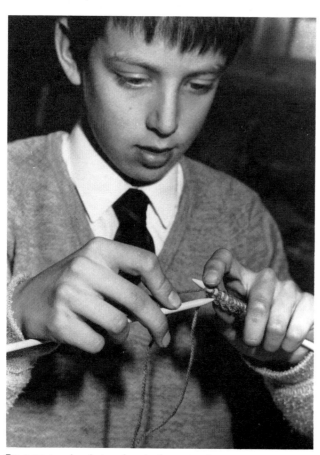

Be sure to check tension before starting.

Abbreviations

There is a standard code of abbreviations used throughout all knitting patterns and books. These will of course vary slightly depending on the individual stitch pattern or design, and each commercial pattern will list the appropriate abbreviations. Here is a list of the ones in common use.

alt	alternate(ly)
beg	begin(ing)
dec	decreas(e/ing)
DK	double knitting yarn
foll	follow(ing)
g st	garter stitch
inc	increas(e/ing)
K	knit
m1	make one stitch
no	number
P	purl
psso	pass slipped stitch over
rem	remain(ing)
sl	slip
sl st	slip stitch
st(s)	stitch(es)
st st	stocking stitch
tog	together

Casting on

There are several methods of casting on depending on the yarn being used or the effect required. The two needle method is the most commonly used but some may find it easier to use the thumb method.

Thumb method

• Make a slip loop 1m from the end of the yarn and slip this on to the needle to be held in the right hand.
• Pass the short length of yarn round the left thumb.
• Insert the point of the needle under the loop on the thumb, and draw forward the long end of yarn from the ball.
• Wind the yarn under and over the needle and draw through a loop, leaving a stitch on the needle.
• Tighten the stitch on the needle, having the yarn round the thumb ready for the next stitch.

Repeat the above steps for the required number of stitches (figure 1).

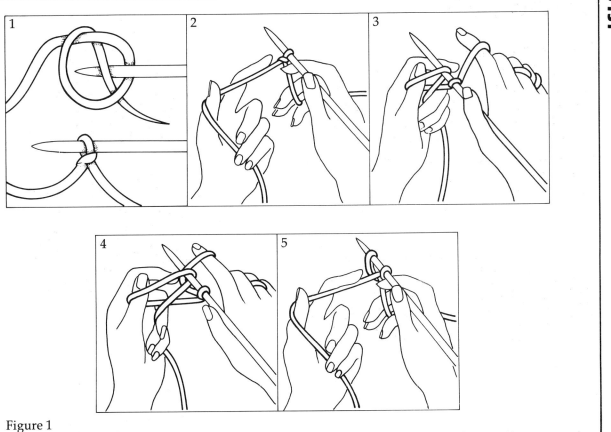

Figure 1

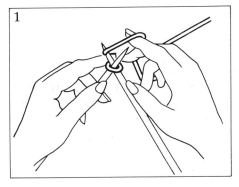

Figure 2

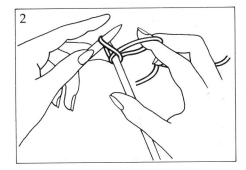

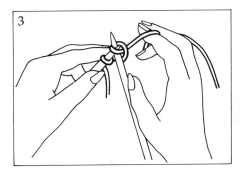

Two needle method

● Make a slip loop about 10 cm from the end of the yarn and slip it on to the needle to be held in the left hand. Insert the right-hand needle into the loop, holding the yarn in the right hand and wind the yarn under and over the needle.

● Draw a new loop through the first loop on the left-hand needle and pass it on to the left-hand needle to form the second stitch.

● Insert the point of the right-hand needle into the last loop on the left-hand needle, wind the yarn under and over the right-hand needle point and draw the new loop through. Slip the new loop on to the left-hand needle. Repeat the movements described in the last step until the required number of stitches have been cast on (figure 2).

Casting off

On a knit row

Knit the first two stitches, then *with the left-hand needle point, lift the first stitch over the second one, leaving one stitch on the right-hand needle. Knit the next stitch and repeat from * until one stitch remains on the left-hand needle. Cut the yarn and draw the end through the last stitch, pulling it firmly (figure 3).

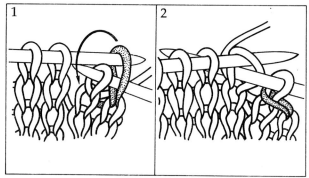

Figure 3

On a purl row

In the case of a purl row, purl each stitch before casting it off. Follow the pattern of the knitting in patterned or rib work as you cast off.

Stitches

Knitting can range from the simplest, plain stitching to the most intricate and complicated pattern combinations but only two basic stitches are used in an endless variety of combinations to create them all: garter stitch (knit stitch) and stocking stitch (purl stitch).

Garter stitch (knit stitch)

• Hold the needle with the cast-on stitches in your left hand. Insert the right-hand needle point from front to back through the first stitch on the left-hand needle.
• With the yarn held behind the needles, pass it round the point of the right-hand needle to form a loop.
• Draw the loop through the stitch on the left-hand needle to form a new loop on the right-hand needle.
• Allow the stitch on the left-hand needle

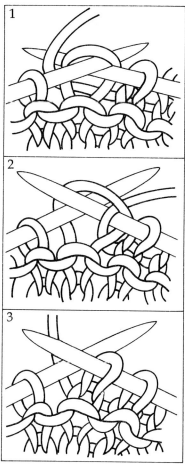

Figure 4

to slip off.

Repeat the first two steps until you have drawn loops through all the stitches on the left-hand needle and passed them on to the right-hand needle (figure 4).

To work the next and following rows, change the needle holding the stitches to your left hand and the free one to your right hand, and work the next row in the same way as the first row.

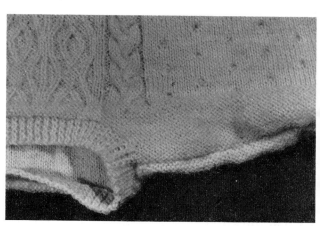

The reverse of stocking stitch shows through as garter stitch.

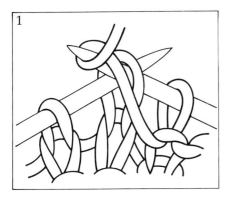

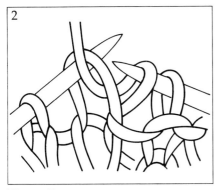

Figure 5

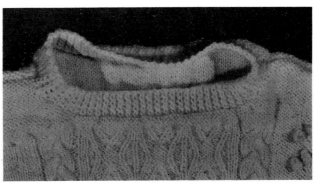

Make complex patterns using garter and stocking stitch.

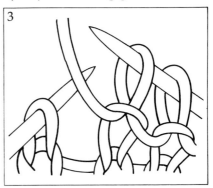

Stocking stitch (purl stitch)

● Hold the needle with the cast-on stitches in your left hand and the other needle in your right hand. Insert the right-hand needle point through the back of the first stitch on the left-hand needle.

● With the yarn towards you, in front of the needles, pass the yarn round the point of the right-hand needle to form a loop.

● Draw the loop through the stitch on the left-hand needle to form a new loop on the right-hand needle.

● Allow the stitch on the left-hand needle to slip off (figure 5).

Repeat the first three steps inclusive with the next stitch until you have drawn loops through all the stitches on the left-hand needle and passed them on to the right-hand needle. Work alternate rows of knit and purl stitch to form stocking stitch.

Joining in a new yarn

The easiest and the best way of joining in a new yarn is at the beginning of a row. A row of stitches will take up at least three times its length in yarn, so you can judge when you will need a new yarn. Simply drop the old yarn at the end of the row and begin the next row with the new one. After knitting one row, tie the ends together. Sew the ends in after the work is completed.

Simple stitch patterns

Knit and purl stitches can be combined to make an amazing variety of textures and patterns. A good way to try out these stitches is to knit 10 cm squares which can be joined together to make cushions or blankets.

Single rib

Cast on an even number of stitches.
*K1, P1, repeat from * to end.
Repeat this row for the required length (figure 6).

Single rib.   Figure 6

Double rib

Cast on a number of stitches divisible by 4.
*K2, P2, repeat from * to end.
Repeat this row for the required length

Moss stitch

Cast on an odd number of stitches.
K1, *P1, K1, repeat from * to end.
Repeat this row for the required length
(figure 7).

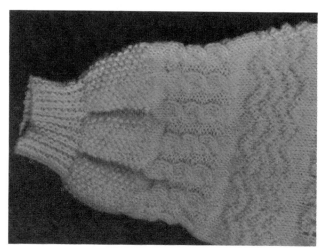

Figure 7   Moss stitch

Double moss stitch

Cast on a number of stitches divisible by 4,
plus 2.
K2, *P2, K2, repeat from * to end.
Repeat this row for required length
(figure 8).

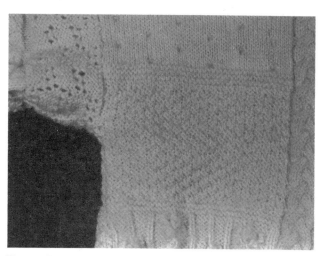

Figure 8   Double moss stitch.
144

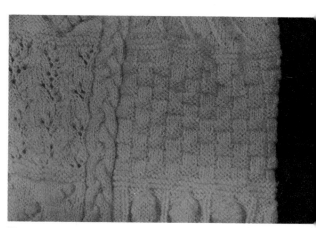

Figure 9   Basket stitch

Basket stitch

Cast on a number of stitches divisible by 8.
1st row. *K4, P4, repeat from * to end.
2nd, 3rd and 4th rows. As first row.
5th row. *P4, K4, repeat from * to end.
6th, 7th and 8th rows. As 5th row.
Continue pattern for required length
(figure 9).

Incorporating decorative items

Beads and sequins

Beads, sequins and other decorative items
such as lengths of plastic tubing, spent ball-
point pens and plastic drinking-straws can
all be chopped into short lengths for
threading on to knitting yarn. Simply thread
the items on to the working yarn and where
you want to place a bead or decoration,
push it up the yarn and knit it in with the
next stitch.

Short lengths of material

To give a shaggy pile texture to pieces of
knitting, cut ribbon, raffia, plastic bags,
fabric or netting into thin strips about 10 cm
long and incorporate them into the work by
knitting them into one or two stitches to
secure them. Trim the strips to the required
length when the work is completed.

Long strips

Weave long strips of ribbon or other
materials into completed pieces of knitting
to create unique textile samples. Exciting
variations can be achieved by weaving into

patterned knitting. Experiment with restricted colour schemes, unusual yarns and materials. The individual pieces of work may be either mounted separately or sewn together to form a wall hanging.

Shaping

A knitted fabric is shaped by either increasing or decreasing the number of stitches. This can be done at the edge of the knitting so that it does not show, or it can be worked as a decorative feature within the main part of the fabric.

Decreasing

To make a simple decrease, work two stitches together, either at the ends of the row or at any other given position.

To decrease one stitch knitwise (K2 tog). Insert the right-hand needle through two stitches instead of one and knit them together. This will slant to the right.

To decrease one stitch purlwise (P2 tog). Insert the right-hand needle through the two stitches and purl them together as one stitch. This will slant to the left.

To decrease using a slipped stitch (sl 1, K1, psso). Slip the first stitch from the left to the right-hand needle, knit the next stitch. With the left-hand needle, lift the slipped stitch over the knitted one and off the needle. This will slant to the left.

This method is used where decreases are paired, one slanting left and one slanting right as on a raglan sleeve, for example.

When you decrease at both ends of a row to form a line that will be seen in the finished work, the lines must be paired so that they slant in opposite directions.

So, when decreasing on the right side of the work, slip 1, knit 1, pass the slipped stitch over (sl 1, K1, psso). These decrease stitches will slant to the left.

At the left-hand end of the row, use a knit 2 together (K2 tog) decrease. These stitches will slant to the right.

This method of decreasing will produce an inward sloping chain effect.

Increasing

The simplest way to increase, is to make an extra stitch at the beginning or ending of a

row. Knit or purl into the stitch in the usual way but do not let it slip off the needle. Instead, insert the right-hand needle into the back of the stitch and knit or purl into it again. Slip both these stitches on to the right-hand needle.

Seams

When stitching pieces of knitting together use a blunt pointed needle such as a tapestry needle as it is less likely to split the threads.

If a fairly thick yarn has been used, either split it or use a thinner matching one for the seams. Heavily textured yarns will also need to be seamed with a finer matching yarn.

Back stitch seam

This makes a strong, firm seam which will help a knitted item retain its shape. Work it in a similar way to that used in dressmaking but check the back of the work to ensure that you are working in a straight line, and not splitting any threads.

Start the seam by working two small stitches one on top of the other, then work back stitch taking care not to pull the stitches too tightly, nor to stretch the seam.

Invisible seam

This seam is stitched from the right side of the work.

Start the seam by securing the sewing yarn to one side. Then work the seam by picking up one loop from alternate sides. After working a few stitches, pull the yarn up firmly so they are not seen on the right side. Continue in this way until the seam is completed.

A simple back stitch seam.   Figure 10

Crochet

Although crochet produces quicker results and is easier to work than knitting, it is less versatile in its uses. Ideally, it looks at its best when worked with the finest of yarns. However, granny squares worked in coloured wools offer an interesting way to experiment with colour combinations, and simple shapes can be quickly worked to make a variety of items.

Yarns

Use any smooth yarn for crochet, including those made from strips of nylon tights and fabrics. Roughly textured yarns are not suitable and hairy ones such as mohair can be difficult to work with. The best thickness of yarn to learn with is either a double knitting or a 4 ply wool. A synthetic or a heavy weight cotton yarn can work up rather firmly, making it difficult to handle. Experiment with a selection of yarns and hook sizes to find the easiest ones.

Hook sizes

ISR hooks

7.00
6.00
5.50
5.00
4.50
4.00
3.50
3.00
2.50
2.00
1.75
1.50
1.25
1.00
0.75
0.60

Abbreviations

Here is a list of the most commonly used crochet abbreviations. You will find further details given with a pattern depending upon the stitches used in the design.

alt	alternate
beg	beginning
ch	chain
dc	double crochet
dec	decrease
dtr	double treble
gr	group
inc	increase
patt	pattern
rep	repeat
RS	right side
ss	slip stitch
sp	space
st(s)	stitch(es)
tr	treble
tr tr	triple treble
WS	wrong side
yrh	yarn round hook

Starting and finishing

All crochet is started with a loop on the hook in the form of a slip knot. To make a slip knot, make a circle with the yarn, holding it in the left hand. Then, keeping the working yarn behind, insert the hook from left to right and pull it through. Tighten the loop on the hook (figure 11).

To finish off the chain or any piece of crochet, break off the working yarn and draw the end through the last loop on the hook.

Stitches

Chain (ch)

Hold the slip knot on the hook with the finger and thumb of the left hand. * Place the hook under the yarn from left to right (yrh), as shown in figure 12. Draw the yarn through the loop already on the hook, making one chain stitch (1 ch). Repeat from * for the required length.

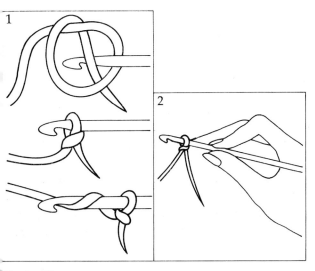

Figure 11

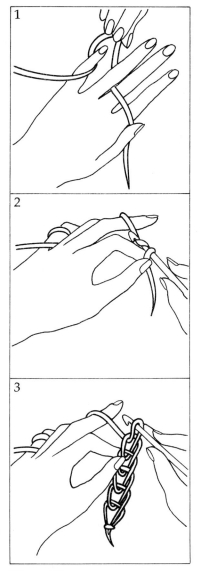

Figure 12

147

Double crochet (dc)

Work the required length of chain plus 2 stitches to turn the chain (figure 13).
1st row * Insert the hook into the top loop of the 3rd chain from the hook. Wrap the yarn round the hook (yrh) and draw it to the front (2 loops on hook). Yrh, then draw the yarn through both the loops on the hook to make 1 double crochet (dc). Repeat from * working the last dc into the turning chain of the previous row.
2nd row 2 ch, * 1 dc into next dc, rep from * working 1 dc into the 2nd of the 2 turning chains.

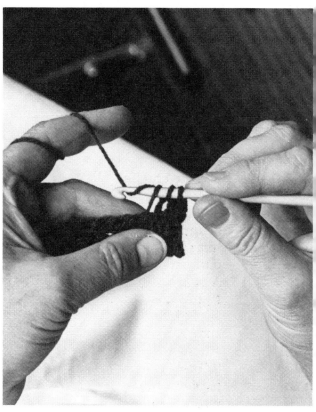

Figure 14

Double treble (dtr)

Work the required length of chain plus 4 stitches to turn the chain.
1st row Miss 4 ch, * yarn twice round hook (y2rh), insert hook into next ch, yrh, draw loop through ch, yrh, draw loop through first 2 loops on hook, yrh, draw loop through last 2 loops on hook and make 1 dtr.
2nd row Work 4 ch. Work 1 dtr into next dtr, rep from * to end of row, working the last dtr into the 4th ch on turning ch. Turn. Rep 2nd row for required length.

Slip stitch (ss)

This stitch is used mainly for making joins in crochet. Work the required number of chain plus 1 stitch to turn the chain.
1st row Miss the 1st ch, * pass the hook through the top loop of the next chain, draw the yarn through, then through the loop on the hook. This makes 1 ss. Rep from * to end of ch.
2nd row 1ch, * 1 ss into next ss, rep from * working the last ss into the turning ch of the last row. Rep 2nd row for the required length. Rep to end of chain.

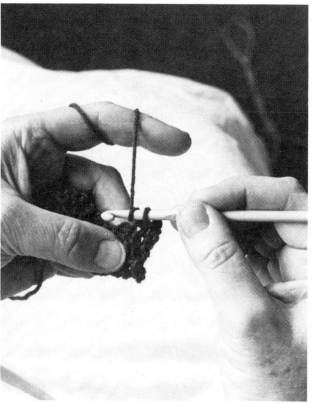

Figure 13

Treble (tr)

Make the required length of chain plus 3 stitches to turn the chain (figure 14).
1st row Miss the first 2 ch, * yrh, insert the hook into the next ch, yrh, draw through 1 stitch (3 loops on the hook), yrh, draw through 2 loops, yrh, draw yarn through remaining 2 loops (1 loop on hook). This makes 1 tr. Repeat from * to end of ch. Turn.
2nd row 2 ch, * 1 tr into next tr, rep from * to last tr, 1 tr into 3rd of 3 turning chain. Turn and rep 2nd row for the required length.

Joining in a new yarn

When only a few centimetres of yarn remain, lay the end along the top of the stitches still to be worked. Join in the new yarn with a slip stitch, work chain stitches to form the first stitch, then work the next stitch and continue working over both thread ends until they are secure (figure 15).

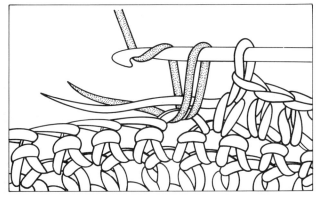

Figure 15

Shaping

Increasing (inc)

The simplest way to increase, is to work two stitches into one at each end of a row, just at one end or at any given place within the piece of work.

The second method is to work as many chain as the number of stitches to be increased. For this method, an increase for the right side of a piece of work is made by adding the extra chain stitches to the end of a wrong side row and vice versa.

Decreasing (dec)

To decrease one stitch at the side, miss the first and last stitches, and when decreasing in the middle of a row, work 2 dc or tr but keep the last loop of each stitch on the hook, then draw a loop through all the loops remaining on the hook.

To decrease several stitches, turn, leaving the number of stitches to be decreased unworked at the end of the row.

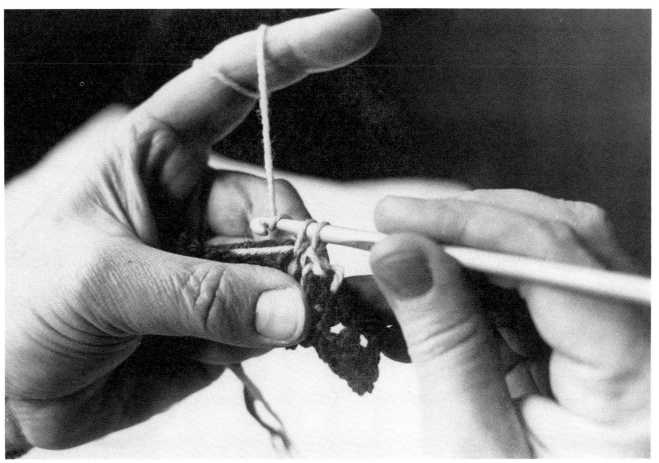

Joining in a new yarn.

Figure 15

Figure 16
Completed granny squares and (inset) starting off a square.

Figure 17

Granny squares

These can be made from scraps of yarn and joined together to make a larger piece of work, provided that yarn of a similar weight has been used for all the squares. They can be made larger if desired, and with several colours (figure 16).

Materials

Yarn in two different colours, a crochet hook.

What to do

Work 4 ch with yarn 1, and join to form a circle with a ss (figure 17).
1st round 3 ch, 2 tr into circle, 1ch, *3tr into circle, 1 ch, rep from * twice. Join into 3rd ch

150

with ss. Break off yarn.
2nd round With yarn 2, join into last sp with ss, 2 ch, 2 tr into same sp, 1 ch, 3 tr into same sp, *3 tr, 1 ch, 3 tr, 1 ch into next sp, rep from * twice, join into 3rd ch with ss. Break off yarn.
3rd round With yarn 1, join into last sp with ss. Continue working groups of 3 tr with 1 ch between along sides, and 2 groups of 3 tr into each corner. Work 3 more rounds in this way.

When enough squares are made, sew them together on the wrong side, or crochet them together, using dc.

Finish the yarn ends by darning them into the same colour yarn so that they are invisible.

Pompons

Pompons will be very popular with the children. They can be used as a trimming to any knitted or crochet fabric.

Materials

Card, a pair of compasses, scissors, yarn, a bodkin.

What to do

Using the pair of compasses, draw two circles on the card measuring the required diameter of the pompon. Cut them out and cut a smaller circle from the centre of each disc.

Place the two discs together and wind yarn round them, using several strands to begin with, then as the hole is reduced in size, use a bodkin until the hole is completely closed.

Using a sharp pair of scissors, insert the point between the two discs and cut through the yarn.

Easing the discs apart slightly, wind and securely tie a length of yarn through the centre of them before easing them away from the pompon.

Roll the pompon between the palms of the hands to firm and shape it. Then trim it to a good shape, leaving the securing yarn for attaching it.

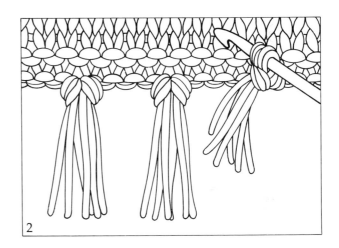

Fringing

This simple form of fringing can be applied to any knitted or crochet fabric as well as to other loosely woven ones (figure 18).

Materials

Yarn, an old book, scissors, crochet hook.

What to do

Wind the yarn round an old book until it is covered. Cut the yarn along one long edge of the book.

Take six strands of yarn, fold them in half, insert the hook into the fabric and draw the loop through. Draw the ends of the yarn through the loop and pull them firmly. Repeat at evenly spaced intervals along the edge.

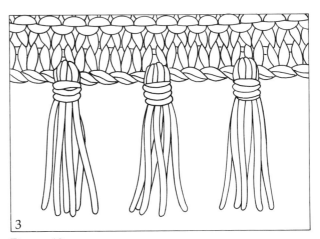

Figure 18

Printing

Printing

INTRODUCTION

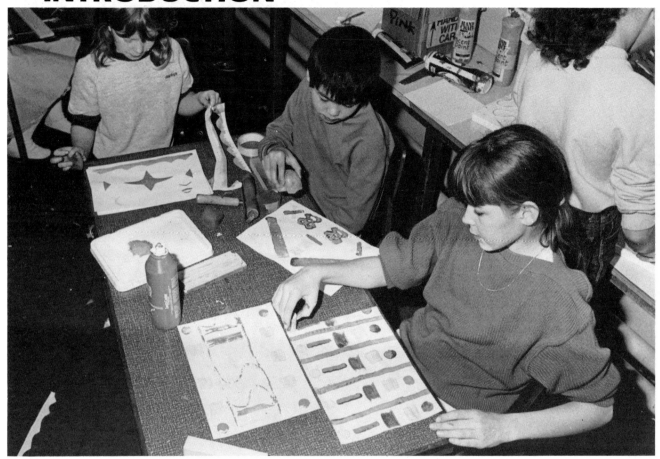

What is a print?

Printing is what happens when ink or paint passes from one surface to another. It can also be said to take place when something firm leaves an impression on something soft – for example, a footprint in sand or a design pressed into soft clay with coins, buttons, cog-wheels or any other decorative shapes.

Using objects to make lasting and distinctive impressions is a very ancient practice: cave paintings include examples of handprints, and one of the oldest forms of writing, Sumerian Cuneiform script, was produced by pressing sticks into clay. Even the fern shapes found on fossils are a form of 'printing by accident'.

Printing has the practical advantage of enabling the same shape to be repeated over and over again. Reading matter, of course, depends upon the repetition of the letters of the alphabet.

Types of printing

There are several types of printing. The ink may be transferred from marks which have been cut into a printing plate as an engraving. Sometimes the ink is transferred from areas left standing after the unwanted parts of a block have been cut away, as in letterpress printing. In lithography, the ink is transferred from marks which have been drawn or photographed on to a flat surface;

and sometimes the ink is forced through the spaces cut in an otherwise impermeable sheet, as in screen printing or stencilling.

It is important not to confuse the children with elaborate technicalities, but to give them opportunities to explore different ways of producing patterns with a variety of objects and materials. Compared with the methods of the professional print-maker, the techniques described here may appear somewhat makeshift, but the experiments are simple and encourage children to be original.

Simple print-making

There is ample scope for craftsmanship in printing, but a simple experimental approach will enable young children to use a variety of implements to make patterns and pictures, which they might not otherwise discover.

Full-scale pictorial print-making is more appropriate for secondary school children who have acquired more ability to use the equipment. However, there are many sorts of simple printing techniques which appeal to younger children. They can be used to produce quick results, and even

those with no taste for drawing can make prints from ready-made or natural objects.

Simple print-making also involves a considerable element of surprise. Unexpected shapes and textures may be produced, and making a printed record of something offers an opportunity to consider its pattern-making possibilities.

Inks and paper

Compared with ordinary drawing inks, printing inks are stickier and slower to dry. You will need a roller and a perfectly smooth slab, such as a piece of firm, smooth plastic, to roll out the ink. Thick plate glass is also suitable, provided that it is very strong and has no sharp edges. Use a separate inking slab and roller for each colour.

Water-based printing inks are recommended for younger children; since both tools and children will be easier to clean. If the ink comes in a tub instead of a tube you will need a spatula or some other means of transferring it to the slab.

Almost any smooth, fairly absorbent paper will serve for printing, although it should not be too thick. Tinted papers can be very attractive.

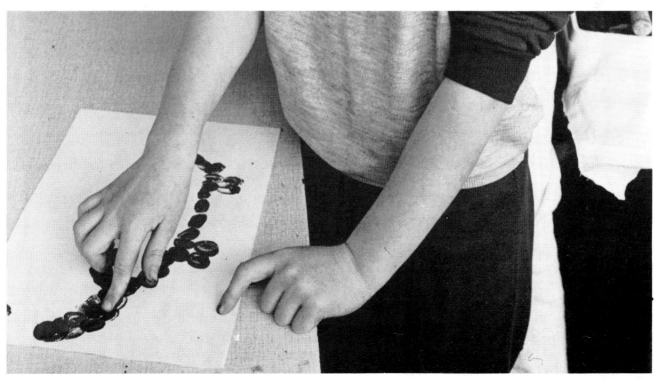

With a little imagination, finger prints can be brought to life.

Impressions from existing things

The use of everyday objects as printing implements can be started in the infant school. It is an easy way to make fairly controlled shapes on paper which can then be embellished or developed as patterns. When children are not preoccupied with making or drawing the shapes, they are better able to concentrate on their composition. Printing the same shape over and over again can help to establish an understanding of rhythm and symmetry.

Fingerprints

Apply a little ink to the slab (see page 159) and roll it out to a thin film. This is best

done by the teacher since children tend to roll out too much.

Press a finger on the ink and then on the paper. It does not take much imagination to bring the prints alive; with the help of a marker pen and a little drawing, fingerprints can grow arms, legs, hats, ears and so on, and animals such as caterpillars can be created.

Footprints

Roll out the ink as before, but this time make sure there is an even covering of ink on the roller. Roll the ink over a shoe sole – preferably one that is not attached to a shoe.

(Shoe soles come in a variety of patterns; choose one with an interesting 'tread'.)

Press the inked sole on to a sheet of paper and stand on it for extra pressure. Then lift the sole away, leaving a print on the paper.

Repeat this process with different colours, allowing them to overlap, or cut out individual prints and mount them on a separate sheet.

Leaf prints.

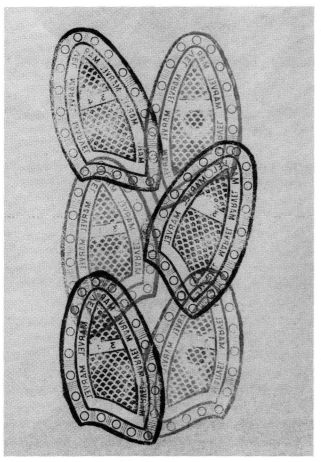

Footprints.

Leaf prints

Collect leaves with a pronounced vein pattern on the underside. Place the leaf on a flat surface, veined side uppermost, and apply ink with a roller. Then position the leaf, inked side down, on a sheet of paper and place another sheet on top. Apply pressure with a clean roller, or place a sheet of cardboard on top and press firmly.

Try composite arrangements, using several leaves together inked with various colours.

Printing from embossed papers

Wallpaper sample books and paper doilies are rich sources of printing material. Old embossed book covers can also be used, but remember that lettering, when printed, will appear back to front.

First cut out shapes from a variety of embossed papers: wallpaper designs are often composed of repeated motifs which lend themselves to this. Assemble the shapes and stick them down on a base sheet, perhaps arranging them to form a picture. Use adhesive sparingly so that there are no lumps.

Other textured materials, such as leather, canvas or coarse fabric, could be incorporated into the design.

When the composition is complete it can be inked with a roller. Then place a sheet of paper on top and apply pressure by hand or with a clean roller.

The children could try making simple posters involving just a few bold words using this technique. Cut out individual letter shapes (back to front) from card or embossed paper. Stick them down making the words appear backwards so that when printed the message comes out the right way round.

Rubbings

Although not exactly a printing technique, making rubbings is certainly an effective means of taking impressions from objects. Since it only requires a sheet of thin paper and a piece of wax crayon, it is less messy than most forms of printing, but it takes a little longer.

Place the paper over the specimen (leaf, doily, book cover, cut-out, or whatever), hold it perfectly still, and make firm strokes with the side of an unwrapped piece of crayon, using black or some dark colour. The crayon shading will almost certainly go beyond the outline of the specimen, so rubbings usually look better when they are cut out and mounted.

Unlike inked impressions, rubbings appear the same way round as the originals, which is convenient when dealing with lettering. They also leave no ink on the specimen itself, so it is a useful method of

Multiple rubbings using wax crayon over card shapes.

recording the textures of tree trunks, brick walls and tombstones.

The children could take impressions using a barely inked roller instead of a crayon. Ink up the roller but remove most of the ink by first rolling it on newspaper, then roll it very firmly over the paper with the specimen beneath.

Subtle background effects can be achieved in this way. Indeed some of the most effective prints are made by combining different techniques.

Printing from blocks

Making a printed impression from some existing object is satisfying enough for young children. Later on, however, they can learn how to use prints to build up deliberate patterns and pictures, and to design and make printing blocks.

Printing units

There are several objects which can be used to print the same shape over and over again. The shape itself may not be very interesting but the speed with which it can be reproduced offers many creative possibilities.

For example, try using polystyrene packaging, pieces of wooden dowel or moulding, erasers, corks and bottle tops. Sometimes these objects can be modified: corks and wooden sticks can be shaped with a file and erasers can be cut with a knife. Potatoes, carrots and other firm vegetables can also be cut to make simple printing units (see page 134).

First apply ink or paint to the object, and then press it on to the paper, so that the shape is transferred or printed.

If small objects are used, apply paint with a brush, and use a thick, opaque watercolour, such as poster colours, tempera colours or powder colours.

For larger objects, roll out some water-based printing ink on a slab and apply it to the object with the roller. Alternatively, pick up ink directly from the slab by pressing the printing implement on to it.

It is best to use a smooth, fairly absorbent paper. A sheet of blotting paper or a flat pad of newspaper underneath may

Bricks printed from an eraser, with paper-cut door and window frames.

improve the printing surface.

Printing implements must be thoroughly washed before changing from one colour to another.

These houses and trees were printed from plastic shapes, a washer and a lollipop stick.

159

Lino cuts

Small lino blocks, no bigger than a matchbox, may also be used as repetitive printing units. These may be cut to interesting shapes or have simple designs cut into them. However, full-scale lino-cutting is not advisable, since it is not easy to cut, and special tools are required.

Lino blocks will last for many printings, and would be suitable for printing repeatedly with oil-based ink on to fabric.

Make sure that the lino is the kind specially supplied for the purpose and secure it to the table with G-clamps before cutting. Children must be taught *always* to use the cutting tools away from themselves.

There are other ways to make simple pictorial blocks for printing which are less durable but easier to prepare.

Polyblock prints

Polyblock is a kind of expanded polystyrene sheet with a smooth surface which will accept printing ink. It is also soft so that indentations can be made easily with various non-cutting implements. A ball-point pen, the end of a brush handle or a modelling tool could be used to 'draw' an indented picture. The block is then inked with a roller and pressed on to paper to make a print.

Some kinds of soft cardboard can be used in much the same way, using an old ball-point pen or a knitting needle.

Blocks from card

Shapes cut from card may be used as printing blocks. If a good quality card with a hard surface is used, several prints can be taken before it begins to wear out. The card should be as stout as possible without being too thick to cut with scissors.

First draw a bold silhouette shape and cut it out. Some shapes look effective when printed repeatedly and overlapped on the same sheet of paper. A forest or a herd of elephants may be built up by printing the same tree or elephant again and again.

Apply ink to the cut-out shape with a roller. Place the shape, ink down, on the

160

printing paper, put a sheet of clean paper on top and press it by hand or with a clean roller. Peel off the card shape carefully and repeat the process in a fresh position. To give an impression of distance, do not re-ink the card – this will give a fainter print.

Try mounting a number of cut-out shapes together on one piece of strong cardboard. Make sure the components are mounted fairly close together, otherwise the background will also pick up ink.

Blocks from modelling material

Prints may even be taken from soft materials such as the various synthetic modelling 'clays'. (Natural clay is unsuitable because it quickly dries and cracks.) Designs tend to distort under pressure so this method is not suitable for repetitive printing. It does, however, produce some unusual textural effects, and can provide starting points for original picture-making.

First make a flat pancake from the modelling material. This must be perfectly smooth, so use a rolling-pin or sandwich the material between two plastic-covered boards or two slabs of strong plate glass. (Be careful when children are using glass: ensure that it is very strong and that the edges are smoothed or taped.)

Cut areas away from the pancake or press into it with bottle tops, pens, paper clips, and other everyday objects, to make a design. Then apply ink with a roller and make a print by laying paper on top and pressing gently.

Another method is to make a composition with 'worms' and pellets of modelling material on a board. Flatten the design by rolling or by pressing carefully with another board or slab of glass. Then print as before.

This sort of activity could never be described as precision printing, and continual applications of ink do not improve the modelling material if you wish to use it later for modelling, but by experimenting with different techniques, children encounter the unexpected and learn to exploit various materials.

Blocks from plaster

Engraved plaster offers opportunities to those who prefer to exercise a little more control over the picture-making process.

First make a plaster block or tile with a very smooth surface, about the size of a postcard (this is less likely to break than a bigger one).

Set up a wall of modelling material about 2½ cm high on a slab of glass or some other very smooth surface. Smear the modelling material down round the outside to make a watertight mould.

Then mix the plaster with water until it has a creamy consistency, and pour it into the mould filling it to the top of the wall. The plaster will set in a few minutes but should be left for an hour or so before removing the wall of modelling material and separating it from the glass (a gentle tap should cause the plaster block to come away). Smooth down any rough edges with coarse sandpaper and leave the block in a warm place for a day to dry out.

The surface of the plaster block could be lightly painted with watercolour before applying the design so that engraved lines will show up more easily.

The picture or pattern could be drawn on tracing paper first, and then transferred to the block. To do this, lay the drawing over the block with carbon paper in between and go over the lines again with a pencil. Watch out for letters and anything else which must be reversed in order to come out the right way round when printed.

Many children, however, prefer to scratch their design directly on to the block, engraving lines by scraping with a nail, knitting needle or some other pointed implement.

The finished engraving may be printed like any other block, but remember that plaster is brittle. Having inked the surface with a roller and placed paper on top, it would be better to put a sheet of card on top of the paper and gently rub with some burnishing implement, such as the handle of a spoon.

If the printing ink is absorbed too quickly by the block, make it less absorbent by applying a coat of size or shellac. Plaster blocks will produce good crayon rubbings, too.

Rotary printing

Another exciting pattern-making experiment involves printing from the surface of a cylinder. A rolling-pin with handles at each end is an ideal implement, but a strong cardboard tube or a plastic container, such as a detergent container, could be adapted. If the cylinder has no handles, restrict the design to the central part so that the two ends may be kept free from ink.

Using the rubber from an old inner tube, cut decorative shapes and stick them securely on to the surface of the cylinder. Fine string or pieces of coarse fabric could also be stuck on, provided that they are all about the same thickness.

Roll the cylinder over an inked slab so that the raised portions pick up an ample supply of ink. Then roll the cylinder over a sheet of paper laid out on a flat surface, exerting enough pressure to transfer the design.

Even without a raised design, some interesting effects may be achieved by applying ink directly from roller to paper. In this case, try intermingling and overprinting different colours.

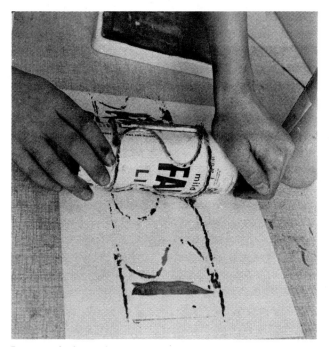

Rotary printing using an old detergent container.

161

Card edge prints

Children are often hesitant about making decisive straight lines with a brush. One way to encourage bold structural painting is to print from the edges of strips of stout card which have been cut with a guillotine or card cutter.

Supply each child with strips of various lengths, some black paint (colour blocks are convenient for this), a brush and a sheet of paper.

Apply paint to the edge of the card and then simply press down on the paper, leaving a strong, slightly splintery line. The card may be held in both hands and bowed to produce a curved line. Corrugated cardboard will produce a crinkly line.

It is possible to build up quite complicated designs fairly quickly with this method, which can be used to make pictures of skeletons, spiders and spiders' webs, cranes, bridges, architectural subjects, and

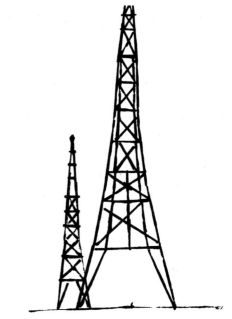

A card edge print.

stained-glass windows. Colour may be added afterwards using paint, crayons or coloured tissue-paper.

Monoprinting

Monoprinting, as the name implies, is not intended to reproduce a design many times. It is a means of preserving on paper a design which has been freely created on another surface. The act of lifting a design from one surface to another can

162

usually be done only once, and the resulting print will have a special texture. Ordinary paints dry too quickly, but printing ink and finger paint are relatively slow-drying and therefore suitable for monoprints.

Finger paint

Finger paint can be made from powder colour mixed to a thick consistency with wallpaper paste, but commercially formulated finger paint is much more reliable and easy to use.

Apply a spoonful of paint to a wet, slippery surface, such as a plastic work-top. The child, wearing an apron and with sleeves rolled up, then makes patterns by smearing it rhythmically in different directions with hands and fingers. The paint can also be moved with sticks, sponges and pieces of card. While the design is still wet, lay a sheet of paper on top, press down evenly with clean hands, and peel it off bearing the printed pattern.

This is a valuable activity, enabling young children to experience the feel of painting on a broad scale. However, it does require space and supervision, and is definitely not recommended for more than a few children at a time.

Variations

For more controlled work, apply printing ink evenly with a roller to a smooth working surface, such as a plate glass slab. Several colours may be intermingled.

Make a cardboard 'comb' by cutting notches at intervals along the edge of a piece of card, and drag this repeatedly across the inked area, leaving a furrowed pattern of straight and wavy lines. Pictures may be drawn using other implements, such as matchsticks, cocktail sticks, pipe-cleaners, straws and scraps of corrugated cardboard.

Work fairly quickly because the ink must not be allowed to dry. A monoprint may then be taken as described above.

For another kind of monoprint first make a simple line drawing in pencil on thin paper. Roll out on to the slab an area of printing ink as large as the drawing, and leave it until it is not quite dry. Then lay the

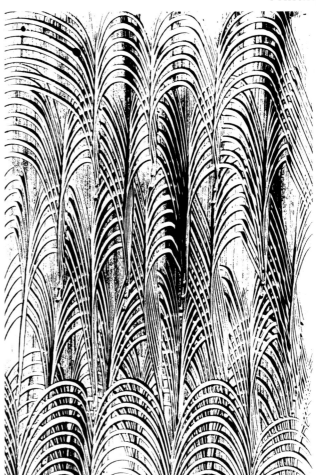

A monoprint from a combed finger painting.

paper gently on top, pencil drawing uppermost, but do not press it down.

Go over the pencil drawing with a ball-point pen or a blunt stick, such as a brush handle, taking care not to press down the surrounding paper. Finally, peel off the paper which should carry a textured version of the original drawing on the reverse.

It may not be too late to take a print of another version of the same picture by pressing a sheet of paper on to the ink left on the slab.

A colourful experiment

Apply a few large drops of brightly coloured water paint on to a slab of thick glass. Place another slab on top and press firmly so that the colours, sandwiched between them, all run together. Then prise the two slabs apart. Suction will cause the paint to form veins

163

and rivulets of colour from which monoprints can be taken.

Oil paint

For more detailed work, a slow-drying oil paint should be used. Any oil painting, provided that it has been done on a hard, smooth surface and is still sticky, may be used for monoprinting.

Stencils

Stencils are a means of masking off some shapes so that paint or printing ink can be applied to the areas around and between. Infants can make simple stencils, but more intricate designs can be very demanding

Paper cuts

Symmetrical paper cuts may be made by cutting shapes from folded paper and then unfolding it. If the paper cut is to be used as a stencil, strong tracing paper is most suitable because it will not soon become soggy and unmanageable.

For more permanent and advanced stencil cutting, use the special oiled paper supplied for the purpose, or drafting film.

Place the stencil in position on the printing paper so that it will not move (it could be attached with drawing-pins). Apply the paint (colour blocks are most convenient) with a small sponge or a scrap of foam plastic (as used in upholstery). Pick up a little paint on the sponge, remove most of the paint by pressing the sponge on newspaper, and then apply it through the stencil to the work with a dabbing movement, gradually building up strength Detailed stencils are often best cut with a pointed knife, cutting through the stencil paper on to a cutting mat. This is not generally recommended in the primary school, except perhaps for some older and more careful children.

of colour. Children tend to allow the stencil and paper to get far too wet, so warn them against this.

To exploit the creative possibilities of stencilling, reposition the stencil again and again, using different colours and allowing them to overprint one on top of another. Each layer of colour must be allowed to dry each time before removing the stencil.

Dabbing paint with a sponge can be rather laborious for large stencils. Spray paints are much quicker, and if there is plenty of space and surrounding areas are adequately protected, they can be used to good effect. However, they are more expensive and can be rather hazardous.

Screen printing

Screen printing is a form of stencil printing. The stencil may consist of several parts which are held together by the screen, and special screen-printing ink is pushed through the screen on to the printing paper with a rubber blade or squeegee. See page 182 for a list of suppliers.

First construct a simple rectangular wooden frame (the components for this may be purchased ready to assemble). Cut a piece of screen-printing mesh about 4½ cm bigger than the frame all round. (A general purpose Terylene mesh is available: this is an extremely fine fabric netting.) Stretch the screen tightly across the frame in both directions, stapling it securely to the wood all round the outside. Mask off a border all the way round underneath with masking tape so that only an inner rectangle of the screen remains clear. The tape border at each end must be wide enough to provide a reservoir for the ink. The screen is then ready for use.

Lay down the printing paper, cut a paper stencil (or several stencils) from strong tracing paper and arrange them on the printing paper, making sure they do not exceed the available area of the screen. Place the screen carefully on top so that it is in contact with the stencil. Pour ink inside the frame along one end. Then, holding the frame steady, draw the ink from one end to the other with the squeegee pressing firmly Remove the frame. The stencil should cling to the underneath of the screen ready for next time, leaving a print on the paper.

For more precise screen printing and for repetitive work, a stencil may be created with light-sensitive emulsion which is fused photographically to the screen. The frame may also be attached to the bench with a special hinge.

Spinning and weaving

Spinning and weaving

INTRODUCTION

We live in a world where machinery is taking over the production of our everyday needs, sometimes depriving us of the satisfaction and sense of achievement gained from making them ourselves. People are therefore becoming more aware of the need to express themselves and to preserve our traditional crafts.

Spinning and weaving helps to fulfil these requirements, whilst providing a range of valuable learning experiences. It encompasses history, environmental studies, science, maths, aesthetic awareness, physical skills, language use and the personal satisfaction of having created something.

An enthusiastic and well-prepared teacher can turn spinning and weaving into a class project for all ages. It can take in all aspects of textile design, from clothing to decorative items, which can be investigated by the pupils through demonstration and exploration. Apart from the skills of spinning and weaving, many other practical skills can be incorporated, such as construction, dyeing, sewing and woodwork (making looms).

Outside sources

Inviting crafts people as guests into the school is an excellent way of introducing spinning and weaving to pupils. The Association of Guilds of Weavers, Spinners and Dyers will be able to give you addresses of local people to contact, and the British Wool Marketing Board will also be able to help you to prepare for the project. See page 182 for further details.

Basic equipment

Most of the hardware for spinning and weaving can be made easily, by either the teacher or the children (depending on age). Although this can be time-consuming it will cut down dramatically on cost, especially when each child needs his or her own equipment.

Spindles

A simple spindle can be made by the children using a round potato and a long pencil (figure 1). The teacher should 'skewer' each potato before the child attempts to push the pencil through.

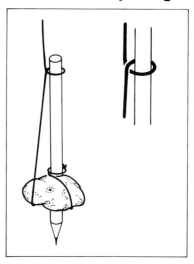

hitch knot

Figure 1

Weaving cards

Use card from old cardboard boxes to make a master card which the children can then use as a template. Be sure that the V shapes

Weaving cards are simple to make, easy to use and cost next to nothing if you use scrap card.

are opposite one another at each end of the card to ensure that the threads lie parallel when the warp is wound on (figure 2).

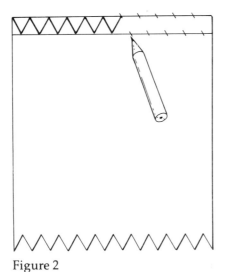

Figure 2

Weaving looms

Old picture frames can be adapted as long as they are flat. These have an advantage over weaving cards since the finished weaving can be removed without leaving ends that have to be tied off (figure 3).

Wools

A good variety of yarns, textured and brightly coloured, can be a motivation in themselves. Store yarns in plastic sweet jars, according to colour, so that the pupils can easily choose the yarns they want, and also have a good guide to 'colour families'. Cut the yarns into lengths of about 60 cm to encourage pupils to use a mixture of hues and textures – grass is never the same colour all over!

Alternative materials

Long thin strips of different materials – ribbon, lace, uncombed fleece, leather, hessian, raffia and even long dried leaves – can all be used for weaving to encourage the use of texture and to add interest to the finished work.

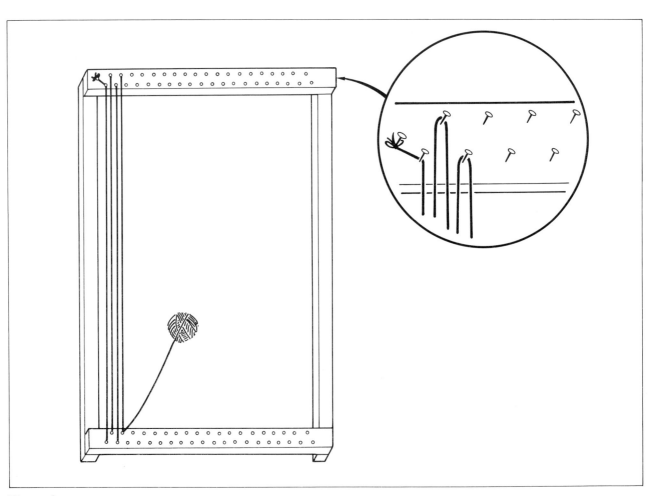

Figure 3

Weaving needles

Plastic needles can be bought quite cheaply – choose long needles which are more able to span the breadth of the weaving.

Shuttles can be made easily, again out of cardboard. Make a template for the children to draw around and cut out (figure 4).

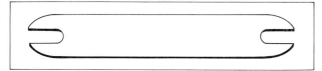

Figure 4

Introducing weaving

It is important that children first learn the correct terminology for the warp and weft. To help them to remember these, point out that the word 'weft' has the 'lines going across' on the letters 'f' and 't'.

An initial investigation of different woven fabrics will demonstrate the principles of weaving. A class discussion can show the children that their clothes are made of 'threads which go in squares, across and down'.

Different fabric samples can demonstrate the strength of tight as opposed to loose weaves (look at hessian and cotton), and the pupils will also be able to see how the weft yarns alternate on each row. When they understand the principles of weave, they can experiment with paper.

Weaving with paper

Weaving with paper is an excellent way to introduce weaving. While mastering weaving methods, the children are using materials which are not only familiar to them but also easier to handle and to pull out if mistakes are made.

Whatever the age of the children, samples of paper weaving should be available for them to refer to while they are working and for you to demonstrate pertinent points. Provide paper already cut into the desired size and demonstrate how to make the warp threads. For younger

children, these could also be ready-made.

Provide each child with an A4-sized sheet of brightly coloured sugar-paper, pencils, a ruler, scissors and glue. Try using magazine pages for weft threads to add variety.

Fold the sugar-paper in half and, beginning at the fold, cut strips stopping short of the top, paper-lantern style (figure 5). Open the paper out.

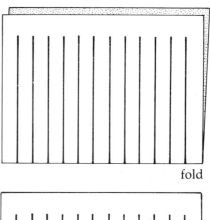

fold

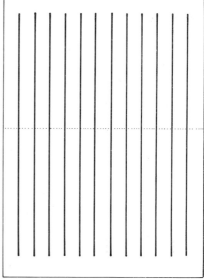

Figure 5   opened out

From another sheet of different-coloured paper or a magazine page, cut individual strips of paper, preferably of a similar size to the warp threads. These can now be woven over and under the warps; a spot of glue at each end will hold them in place.

Some children will weave each line the same as the one before, threading under and over the same warps. This is where you can use the ready-made samples to show how each line alternates, first under, then over, then under etc. This type of weave is known as plain or tabby weave.

Once the pupils have mastered this, more advanced weaves, such as twill and hopsack, can be introduced, depending on the age of the children (figure 6).

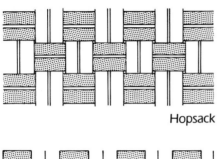

Hopsack

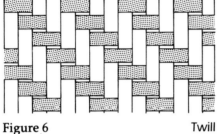

Figure 6   Twill

Follow-up

Older children may like to experiment by altering the spacing between the warps, either by cutting the strips in different

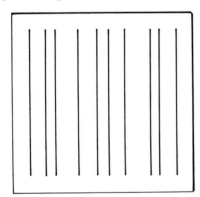

Figure 7

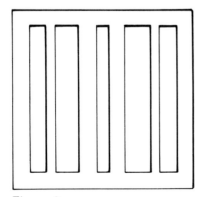

Figure 8

widths (figure 7) or by cutting out alternate warps (figure 8).

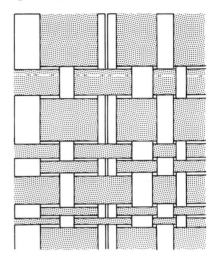

Figure 9

They could also experiment with weft threads, again by using irregular widths (figure 9) or by cutting them in wave shapes. Keep the 'wave' wefts in the same order so that they fit back together, rather like a line jigsaw.

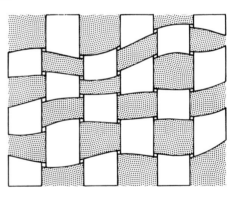

Once these basic weaves have been mastered, the skills can be more easily applied to yarns. The great variety of results will make a wonderful display, and the finished sheets may also be used to prompt written work to accompany the craft work.

Spinning

Let the children handle fleece and wool before spinning.

Having been introduced to woven fabric and paper weaving, the children can discuss the limitations of paper: ie it is stiff, it cannot be easily shaped, the strips slide about etc. The advantages of yarns will then become clear and, by using fleece, they can learn how threads are made.

Begin with a brief introduction about the origin of wool – sheep, shearing and so on. The Wool Marketing Board is a good source of information, depending on the amount of detail that is to be covered. Samples of fleece for the children to look at and handle will familiarise them with the lanolin that is present in the fibres.

Preparing to spin

Either the teacher or a guest 'spinner' should demonstrate the main principles of spinning before the children attempt anything themselves – beginning with the raw fleece, combing and forming 'rolags' (a film of fibres combed and rolled ready for spinning), followed by the spinning process using a spindle. Younger pupils can be shown how to hand-spin fleece by twisting the fibres with their fingers.

When the children are ready to begin, give them a piece of unwashed fleece with a long staple (natural length of a lock of fleece), as this is easier for pupils to handle. They should also have a dog-comb or hand-carder, and a spindle.

To prepare the fibres for spinning, take a handful of the fleece and gently tease the fibres slightly apart, then hold it firmly in one hand, allowing the majority to protrude. Gently comb it to align the fibres and remove any bits.

Fleece with a shorter staple will need to be carded. Again, the fibres must first be teased apart, then placed on to the left-hand carder. (This should be marked on the back with an 'L' so that the carders are not damaged by being used in different directions.) Rest the carder on one knee with the handle pointing away from you and gripped from underneath. The right-hand carder should then be drawn across the left gently towards you. This process should be carried out about six times, until the fibres begin to align and even out.

Next transfer the remainder of the fibres from the left-hand carder on to the right using the following method. Without changing the position of your hands on the handle, turn the right-hand carder to face upwards. Put the bottom edge of the left-hand carder to the handle edge of the right-hand carder and move them in opposite directions pressing firmly, thus enabling the fibres to be transferred from one to the other.

Carding is then resumed in the original position. Once this process has been followed a few times and all the fibres are aligned, they can be removed and rolled into a rolag or long tube shape ready for spinning.

How to use a spindle

To prepare the spindle, tie a length of strong woollen yarn on to the shaft near the base of the spindle, hitch it once round the underside of the base, then loop it with a hitch knot about 2.5 cm from the top (or in the notch if it is a ready-made spindle). Allow about 30 cm of thread to extend upwards.

Take a rolag of fleece, tease out a few of the fibres at one end and overlap this with the end of the yarn on the spindle. Hold them both with one hand (normally the left hand) and allow the spindle to hang free. With the other hand twist the spindle clockwise by gripping the top and giving it a sharp flick. Move this hand quickly back up to grip the join. Pull the left hand gently upwards to allow more fibres to be drawn out and allow the twist to run up on to these fibres by releasing the hold of the lower hand (right hand).

Although this process sounds quite complicated, it is amazing how quickly pupils grasp the concept and produce yarns with a wonderful texture!

Once a long length of thread has been

Carders are used to align the fibres for spinning.

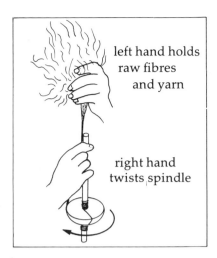

left hand holds
raw fibres
and yarn

right hand
twists spindle

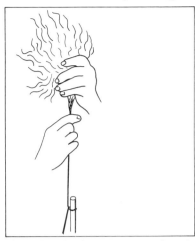

Once the spindle is spinning, move the right hand up to pull the fibres from the rolag.

produced, unhitch it and wind it on to the shaft, then re-hitch the thread leaving about 15 cm of yarn extending. Then repeat the whole process.

Finger spinning

Younger pupils or those without spindles can twist yarns with their fingers.

Comb the fibres first, then draw them out as before, twisting them between the finger and thumb. Pupils can work in pairs, drawing out all the fibres then each gripping one end and both turning to the right, starting in the middle and working towards the ends.

A variety of yarns can be created using hand-spun or commercially produced yarns.

Yarns can be plyed by twisting a pair in the opposite direction (figure 10). One end can be tied on to a chair back or held by one

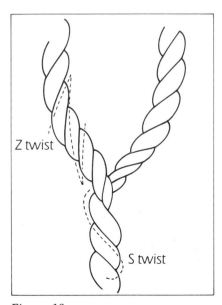

Z twist

S twist

Figure 10

Using a spindle to twist the fibres into yarn.

175

child while another one twists.

This method can also be used to make thicker yarns with commercially produced wool, perhaps adding extra interest by mixing textures and/or colours.

Yarns can also be plaited, or knotted to make slubs, and finally dyed to finish off.

Display the yarns

The yarns may now be kept ready for weaving. Display them for pupils to see what has been produced and to explain to the rest of the group how they achieved the different effects.

Weaving

Once the children have learned the weave techniques from paper weaving, they can move on to weaving fabric.

Use a partly woven sample to explain the problems that might be encountered with the selvages (the cloth border which cannot be unravelled): ie if they pull on their weft threads too hard, the selvages will begin to bow inwards, thus spoiling the shape of the weaving. Ask the children to suggest ways of avoiding this: they could either draw the last warp thread, or hold the warp thread in position while tightening the weft. They also need to be shown the importance of leaving enough thread at the beginning and the end of each yarn to finish off.

Using yarns of different colours and textures adds interest to the weaving. Point

out that everything has a texture, and encourage the children to describe the texture of objects they see around them or in photographs – whether it is bumpy, smooth, spiky, prickly, rough, and so on. Then explain how they can find or make threads which match these textures.

It is best to start with a simple weaving project, such as a small picture, which can be finished fairly quickly using only short lengths of yarn to avoid tangles.

Weaving cards and metal frames

Weaving cards may be prepared as shown in figure 11. This type of weaving will need to be finished off when it is removed from

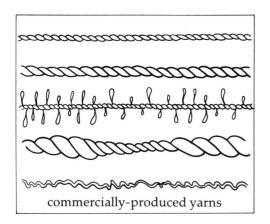

commercially-produced yarns

the card.

If time and money are available, try making a small metal frame. This can be used as both a loom and a picture frame, and is ideal for small woven pictures. It also eliminates the problem of an uneven selvage, as the sides of the frame can be treated as the end weft threads.

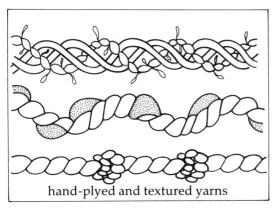

hand-plyed and textured yarns

Make the frames as shown in figure 12 using wire (about coat-hanger thickness), solder and a soldering iron or yarn to secure the corners.

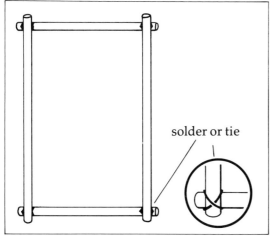

solder or tie

Figure 12

The next step is to 'warp up' the card or loom. A smooth yarn such as waxed string is ideal, especially if textured yarns are being used for the weft threads, as they can be pulled across more easily on the waxed surface. The yarn should not be too thick (3-ply is best) or it will be too noticeable when the weaving is finished.

Each pupil can warp up his or her own card or loom as shown in figure 13. The warp threads on the frames should be evenly spaced, then secured at the top and bottom with a strip of clear sticky tape to hold the threads in place while the pupil is weaving.

A long tail of thread should be left at either end of the card to tie off when the warping is complete.

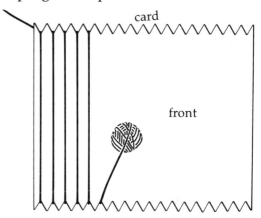

card

front

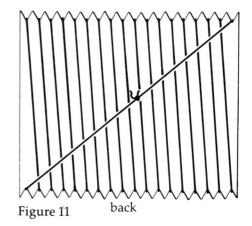

Figure 11   back

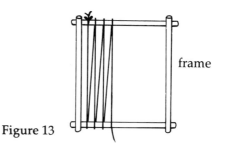

frame

Figure 13

177

Preparing the design

Next, each child needs to draw a small picture as a guide for weaving. First draw a square 1 cm smaller than the inside dimensions of the frame or card (12 cm by 10 cm is a good size). Draw the picture inside this square, keeping it simple, and colour it in (figure 14).

Figure 14

Now draw another square the same size, and this time draw just the background, showing the areas to be woven. Figure 15 shows a simplified background and the order of weaving. Keep the original picture as a reference.

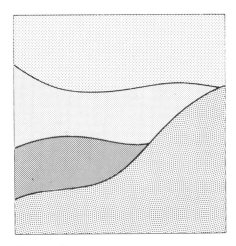

Figure 15

Cut out the square showing the background and slide it behind the warp threads on the card or loom so that it shows through. This will not only act as a guide,

178

but will also prevent the pupils from picking up the rear threads by mistake if they are using a frame.

Starting to weave

The children can now begin to weave, starting at the bottom right-hand corner and remembering to leave extra thread at the end for finishing off. The teacher should help with the first two rows to reinforce the technique – weaving rows alternately, taking care at the selveages, leaving thread for finishing off, and so on.

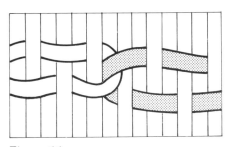

Figure 16

Encourage them to experiment with colour and texture: for example, if area 1 on the background is all green, suggest that the child works in bands of various types of green thread. Where the background changes colour (eg from area 1 to area 2), the child should weave across until he comes to the join, then turn and go back until area 1 is completely filled in. Area 2 is then started from the left-hand side until it meets area 1. They must take care to interweave the join so that there is no gap (figure 16).

Help with the first two rows as children start to weave.

Finishing off

Once the weaving is complete, it can be left on the metal frame, but the weaving should be removed from a card loom. This is done by cutting along the middle of the rear threads and securing them in pairs to prevent fraying (figure 17). Side threads can be sewn in at the back.

Figure 17

The details in the picture, such as the tree and the sun, can now be added using appliqué and stitchery. Encourage the children to use appropriate fabrics: ie coarse, bumpy fabric such as tweed for the bark, and smooth, shiny satin for the sun. Beads and sequins, seeds, leather, wood shavings and anything else you have in the 'scraps bin', can be glued on to build up the final picture.

A weaving loom for larger pieces

A simple weaving loom as shown in figure 18 can be either made or bought. It is more durable than cards or metal frames, and can be used for weaving larger items.

Large-scale weaving is a good opportunity to explore the use of different weaves and yarn thicknesses, and a greater variety of materials. However, it is not so easy to use a background guide (a drawn picture placed behind the threads), although it is possible to lay a guide down underneath the frame if necessary.

A freer style of weaving is better suited to weaving frames. The pupil can work out roughly on paper the form that the weaving will take, but should not depend on reproducing an exact replica.

This type of frame is probably the

easiest to warp up. Tie the warp yarn to the first top left-hand nail and, moving from top to bottom and back again, wind the thread around each nail, tying it off on the last one.

The weaving will not fray at the top and bottom, and lengths of dowelling can be pushed through the loops that are left when the weaving is lifted off the frame to give you a ready-made wall-hanging.

Wall-hangings

The whole class can join together to make a large-scale woven wall-hanging. Fix two pieces of wide dowelling (obtainable from a builders' merchant) about 1.2m apart using table clamps. Wind a heavyweight warp, such as jute or thick string, from one dowel to the other. Suspend this structure from wall brackets, an unused doorway, or anything that leaves space at the back.

The children can then make thick weft yarns by cording, plaiting or plying, or use heavier materials such as long narrow leaves or long plant stems, each child contributing a line of weaving. The results are usually quite stunning!

Circular weaving

A simple circular frame can be made using a lampshade ring.

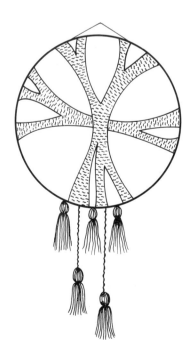

Figure 18

179

Bind the ring all around using strips of fabric or bias binding, then put warp threads across diagonally as a base for needle-weaving. This type of weaving, left on the frame, can make interesting mobiles. If the children use different-sized rings, some can be combined to make large mobiles.

If the weaving is to be removed from the frame, special circular weaving frames should be used, which have small pegs all around the circumference. The warp is wound on in a similar manner to the weaving frame in figure 18. The finished weaving can then be lifted off, and the circles joined together if desired.

The background material

Encourage the children to experiment without constraints, once they have grasped the basic procedure. If they can work without being inhibited, they will produce some interesting and original results.

Using ready-made open-weave fabrics, pupils can explore weft stitches on a more substantial background. Hessian, builder's scrim or rug canvas can be stretched out across a flat wooden frame as a background for weft stitches. Open knitting can be used in the same way.

Thin strips of warp fabric can be pinned to a frame and woven across with more strips in a toning or contrasting colour. The edges of the strips could be frayed to add texture. Chicken wire and garden mesh also make good background materials.

Varying stitches for textural effects

Although they can use different materials to obtain textural effects, older or more proficient pupils may become bored with plain hopsack and twill weaves. So introduce them to different stitches to add further interest to their designs.

Needle-weaving

This can be used in the middle of a design to suggest tree shapes or the stems of plants. Here, the pupils can forget the rule about not pulling the weft yarn across too tightly (figure 19).

Figure 19

Waving

Lines of weaving can be pulled apart and filled with a different stitch or coloured wool (figure 20).

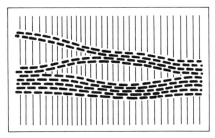

Figure 20

Soumak stitch

This consists of one row of plain weave, then one row of loops. The line of plain weave serves to hold the looped row in place (figure 21).

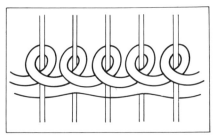

Figure 21

Rya knot

This can be worked using one weft yarn, or a number of yarns at the same time to build up thickness more quickly (figure 22).

Displaying the work

All completed work should be carefully finished and displayed for maximum impact. This can be done in a number of ways.

Small pictures can be displayed in a frame or a small wall-hanging.

Cut out a card picture frame in toning colours to complement the threads used, and glue it over the top of the weaving. Instead of just cutting out square and rectangle shapes, try 'window frames' in the shape of church windows, ovals, circles, and so on.

To make a hanging, tie the threads around a piece of dowelling at the top and bottom, and add a length of thread to hang the picture.

A few ideas are illustrated below.

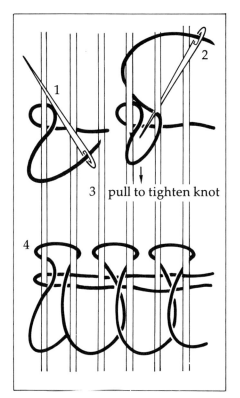

Figure 22

3 pull to tighten knot

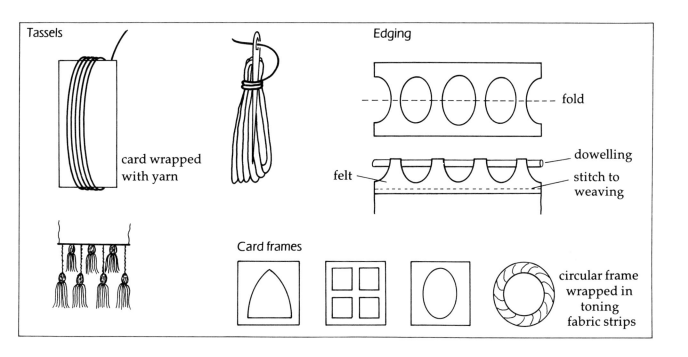

Tassels

card wrapped with yarn

Edging

fold

felt

dowelling

stitch to weaving

Card frames

circular frame wrapped in toning fabric strips

Resources

Books

Teaching Art to Young Children Rob Barnes (Allen & Unwin 1987).

Children and Art Teaching Keith Gentle (Croom Helm 1984).

Art Learning and Teaching Dairmuid Larkin (Wolfhound Press 1981).

Teaching Art in Primary Schools Geoff Rowswell (Bell & Hyman 1983).

Art Techniques for Children Gottfried Tritten (Van Nostrand Reinhold 1964 *op*).

An Eye on the Environment: an Art Education Project H B Joicey (Bell & Hyman 1986).

Learning through Drawing (Art Advisers' Association 1987).

Children's Drawing J Goodnow (Fontana/ Open Books 1977).

Needlework School The Embroiderers' Guild Practical Study Group (Windward 1984).

The Constance Howard Book of Stitches Constance Howard (Batsford 1979 *op*)

Batsford Book of Embroidery Stitches Anne Butler (Batsford 1979 *op*).

Embroidery Stitches Barbara Snook (Dryad 1985).

The Craft of Hand Spinning E Chadwick (Batsford 1980).

Have You Any Wool? J Messent (Search Press Ltd 1986)

Fun with Wool (F Muller Ltd 1983, obtainable from the Knitting Craft Group. PO Box 6, Thirsk, N Yorks YO7 1TA).

All about Fabrics S Holland (Oxford University Press 1985).

All about Weaving C Creager (Robert Hale 1987).

Introducing Finger Painting Guy Scott (Batsford 1973 *op*).

The Art of Stencil Laliberte and Mogelon (Van Nostrand Reinhold 1972 *op*).

Introducing Screen Printing Keith Hughes (E J Arnold).

The Grammar of Ornament Owen Jones (Studio Editions).

Pattern Design Lewis F Day (B T Batsford *op*).

An Illustrated Dictionary of Ornament Dora Ware and Maureen Stafford (George Allen & Unwin *op*).

op Book is no longer in print, try library.

Materials

All the materials and equipment mentioned in this book can be obtained from:

Dryad,
PO Box 38,
Northgates,
Leicester LE1 9BU.

James Galt & Co Ltd,
Brookfield Road,
Cheadle,
Cheshire SK8 2PN.

Nottingham Educational Supplies,
17 Ludlow Hill Road,
West Bridgeford,
Nottingham NG2 6HD.

Weaving equipment, wools, dyes and fleece are available from Kineton Gallery, Kineton, Warwickshire. Send an sae for price lists.

Square, triangular, hexagonal and dot lattice gridsheets are produced by Excitement in Learning, 88 Mint Street, London SE1 1QX.

Organisations

British Wool Marketing Board,
Oak Mills,
Station Road,
Clayton,
Bradford BD14 6JD;
tel 0274 882091.
(Produces packs for teachers; write or phone
for details.)

Association of Guilds of Weavers, Spinners
and Dyers,
c/o Five Bays,
10 Stancliffe Avenue,
Marford,
Wrexham,
Clwyd.
(Will put you in touch with your local
guild).

About the authors

Eileen Lowcock studied fashion and design at Bromley College of Art in the 1950s. She ran her own dressmaking business for ten years, taught adult education classes (dressmaking and tailoring) in Beckenham and Ealing, and was technical crafts adviser to the National Federation of Women's Institutes for three and a half years (a Government Development Commission post). For the past 18 years as a journalist, Eileen has worked on partworks, national magazines and books. (For the last five years as Editor of *Art & Craft*.) She has also written books on embroidery and dressmaking.

Eileen Lowcock, our consultant, is Editor of Art & Craft.

Malcolm Appleby has taught in primary schools in Cleveland for the past 14 years. As well as his teaching qualifications he has a Bachelor of Arts degree, a Master of Arts in Education Degree and a Certificate in Primary Art Education. He has been involved in a wide range of in-service training courses for teachers, both for the local authority and for Teesside Polytechnic, and has taught on an initial teacher training course at the University of Durham. His wife, Sue, is a primary school teacher, and they have two children, Tim and Emma.

Clive Butler started teaching in 1974 after qualifying from St Martin's College, Lancaster. He first taught in several London schools during which time he completed his MA(Ed) in curriculum studies. In 1985 he moved to West Sussex to take up his first headship, and he is now a regular contributor to *Art & Craft* magazine.

Mary Lack, after gaining a diploma in graphic design and completing a post-graduate teaching course, taught in various schools and further education establishments. She now teaches part time and works as a free-lance writer, designer and illustrator.

Wendy Hawkin has a first degree in art education and an MA, and has been teaching full time in Buckinghamshire schools for the past ten years. A textile artist, she exhibits regularly and has work in public and private collections in this country and abroad. She also lectures on embroidery and textiles and runs workshops around the country.

Pauline Rayner came into teaching via the industrial world, having studied electrical and mechanical engineering for two years in her late teens. At teacher training college she studied the art of movement, looking at all aspects of dance, in terms of harmony, form, dynamics and rhythm. She now teaches at Longfield Middle School, where she combines practicality and harmony in using many materials, so that when children make coil pots, they also make a small wooden ornament shelf supported by a mild steel bracket. Most of the work she has developed on pottery at Longfield is a result of numerous pottery classes and visits to fine arts and ceramics exhibitions in London, Spain, France, Italy, Greece, Germany and Yugoslavia.

Mary Smart, currently deputy head at Magdalen Gates First School, Norwich, has been teaching four- to eight-year-olds for more than ten years, including three years at an Observation and Assessment Centre and the remainder in First Schools with the exception of a year teaching a middle school class of nine- and ten-year-olds. She has been involved in part-time youth work, play schemes and children's camps, and has also compiled *Bright Ideas Christmas Activities.*

Maureen Greenland is a regular contributor to *Art & Craft* magazine. She taught three- to eight-year-olds in London and Canada before becoming a polytechnic lecturer in professional studies, teaching BEd students. Now a free-lance writer with a special interest in the subject of pattern, she enjoys working informally with children. Probably the only quill pen maker known to the taxman, Maureen founded the Writing Equipment Society, and international society for collectors. She is also engaged in historical research and is at present helping to restore two early nineteenth century printing machines for a museum.

Chris Vesey is a lecturer in fashion and textiles at Mid Warwickshire College of Further Education. She trained at Liverpool and Sheffield Polytechnics and has been teaching at various levels since 1976. Chris finds working with dyes and fabrics stimulating both as a fashion medium and as a teaching tool. The element of experimentation and discovery in this work is, she feels, particularly valuable to younger children. 'Older children always enjoy textiles work, and what better way to teach and reinforce basic colour theory and mixing? Whatever the capabilities or limitations of a child, they will achieve pleasing and colourful results by following only the simplest instructions.'

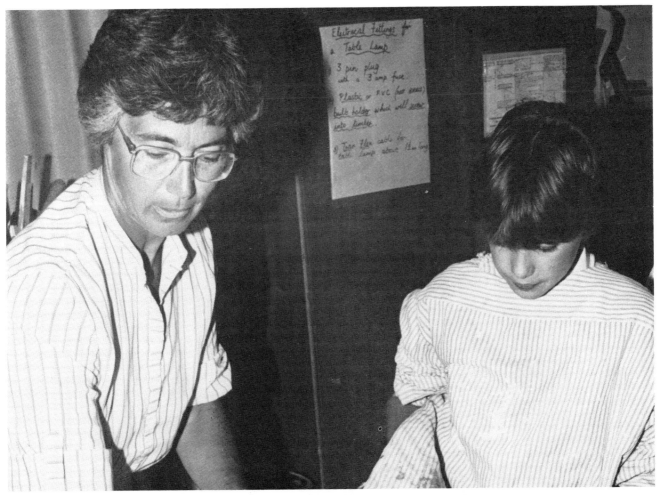

Pauline Rayner attempts to combine practicality and aesthetic appeal in her clay work.

Roland Smith has 30 years' experience of primary and secondary education, specialising in art and craft, and was most recently head of the junior department at Cannock School, Kent. He has written several craft books, and has often contributed to educational journals in the UK and in America. Many of his own prints and pictures have appeared as reproductions, published by Athena International and others, and have been widely used in schools. He now teaches calligraphy and works as an illustrator and design consultant. He is a chartered designer and an ordinary fellow of the College of Preceptors. He has designed educational games and equipment for E J Arnold, and is chiefly concerned with the creative work of young children, which he sees as a process of exploration and discovery.

Roland Smith, author of the 'Printing' chapter.

Sandra Goode helps a pupil with weaving.

Sandra Goode learned embroidery from her German aunts and grandmother at the age of seven. She trained at Bournville Art College, then Hereford College of Education, specialising in art and design. After teaching in Birmingham for one year, she worked as a free-lance press and publicity agent in London for three years, then returned to Birmingham and teaching. Having recently completed three years in-service BEd (Hons) at Birmingham University, she is now teaching textile design at Holte School, Lozells.

Index

Acknowledgements

Chace Junior School, Coventry; SS Mary &
John CE First School, Oxford; Coton End
Middle School, Warwick; Courthouse Green
Junior School, Coventry; Holte Secondary
School, Birmingham; Longfield Middle
School, Harrow; St Mary's CE Junior School,
Hornsey, London; Arts for All, Coventry;
Art & Craft magazine for 'Girl and horse'
collage.

Other Scholastic books

Bright Ideas

The *Bright Ideas* books provide a wealth of resources for busy primary school teachers. There are now more than 20 titles published, providing clearly explained and illustrated ideas on topics ranging from *Writing* and *Maths Activities* to *Assemblies* and *Christmas Art and Craft*. Each book contains material which can be photocopied for use in the classroom.

Teacher Handbooks

The *Teacher Handbooks* give an overview of the latest research in primary education, and show how it can be put into practice in the classroom. Covering all the core areas of the curriculum, the *Teacher Handbooks* are indispensable to the new teacher as a source of information and useful to the experienced teacher as a quick reference guide.

Management Books

The *Management Books* are designed to help teachers to organise their time, classroom and teaching more efficiently. The books deal with topical issues, such as *Parents and Schools* and organising and planning *Project Teaching*, and are written by authors with lots of practical advice and experiences to share.